"Few, if any, books are built on such a solid base of evidence as this gem. If the goal is to truly manage social anxiety and experience a richer life, this is what you need."

—**Todd B. Kashdan, PhD**, author of *The Art of Insubordination*; and professor of psychology who leads The Well-Being Laboratory at George Mason University, USA

"If you struggle with social anxiety and are looking for an easy-to-understand, no-nonsense, effective self-help book, then *CBT for Social Anxiety* by Stefan Hofmann is the book for you. Based on decades of research and written by one of the foremost experts in the field, *CBT for Social Anxiety* is an essential volume for anyone seeking to learn proven techniques for understanding and overcoming their anxiety in social situations."

—**David A. Moscovitch, PhD, CPsych,** professor of psychology at University of Waterloo, Canada

"Social anxiety is a painful and debilitating condition affecting many people. Some of them are too shy to come to treatment. The new book by Stefan Hofmann is a gift for these individuals. The book incorporates cutting-edge research as well as ancient wisdom in a readable, engaging manner. It is filled with personable, real-life examples. I can envision many people turning to this book for insight, advice, and inspiration."

—**Eva Gilboa-Schechman**, professor of psychology at Bar-Ilan University in Israel

T0026594

"An engaging book that provides a clear and detailed path to overcoming social anxiety. Hofmann presents helpful illustrations, case examples, and activities that will help people understand and reduce their social fears. Family and friends of socially anxious people will also benefit from reading this comprehensive guide."

—**Lynn E. Alden, PhD**, professor and clinical psychologist
at The University of British Columbia in Canada

"This book brings together Hofmann's vast scientific knowledge of debilitating social anxiety with his warmth and humanity to create a pearl of a volume that will speak directly to all sufferers of this widespread problem. Practical skills and strategies, experience-based examples, along with clear and easy-to-read writing make this a book that holds tremendous importance to all people who are serious about mastering their social anxiety."

—**Ronald M. Rapee, PhD**, distinguished professor of
psychology at Macquarie University in Australia,
and author of *Overcoming Shyness and Social Phobia*

"Stefan Hofmann, a pioneer in the treatment of social anxiety, provides us with an inviting and inspiring set of tools and practices that have been proven helpful. This is a must-read for anyone who is troubled by, lives with, or treats someone with social anxiety."

—**Murray B. Stein, MD, MPH, FRCPC**, distinguished
professor of psychiatry and public health at the University
of California, San Diego

CBT
for
Social
Anxiety

Simple Skills for
Overcoming Fear and
Enjoying People

STEFAN G. HOFMANN, PHD

New Harbinger Publications, Inc.

NEW HARBINGER PUBLICATIONS is a registered trademark of New Harbinger Publications, Inc.

New Harbinger Publications is an employee-owned company.

Copyright © 2023 by Stefan G. Hofmann

New Harbinger Publications, Inc.
5674 Shattuck Avenue
Oakland, CA 94609
www.newharbinger.com

Cover design by Amy Shoup; Acquired by Elizabeth Hollis Hansen; Edited by Rona Bernstein

Library of Congress Cataloging-in-Publication Data

Names: Hofmann, Stefan G., author.
Title: CBT for social anxiety : simple skills for overcoming fear and enjoying people / Stefan G. Hofmann.
Description: Oakland, CA : New Harbinger Publications, [2023] | Includes bibliographical references.
Identifiers: LCCN 2023002970 | ISBN 9781648481208 (trade paperback)
Subjects: LCSH: Social phobia. | Cognitive therapy.
Classification: LCC RC552.S62 H653 2023 | DDC 616.89/1425--dc23/ eng/20230203
LC record available at https://lccn.loc.gov/2023002970

Printed in the United States of America

25   24   23

10   9   8   7   6   5   4   3   2   1   First Printing

To my sons, Benjamin and Lukas.

Contents

Foreword

Human nature is often filled with contradictions, and social anxiety is one of them. We have evolved to want connection with others, but at the same time we fear the rejection that might come. How can we make sense of this and how can we overcome our fears of being negatively evaluated—or humiliated? Hofmann helps us understand that we are not alone. Even celebrities can suffer from social anxiety disorder.

Thirteen percent of us will at some time suffer from social anxiety disorder, making it one of the most common psychological problems that people have. Many aspects of life are affected by this kind of anxiety, including the ability to advance in your career, make and maintain friendships, and find a partner. Often the limitations of social anxiety will lead to depression as people feel less effective, more self-critical, and often hopeless. Many will turn to alcohol and drugs to cope with the stress.

Professor Stefan Hofmann is one of the world's leading authorities on anxiety. His research program over many years has covered almost every aspect of psychological difficulties people confront, and his work on social anxiety disorder has direct application to helping people overcome this often troubling and all-too-common problem.

When I read a book, I ask myself, what questions will this book answer? Here are some questions you can keep in mind as you read this book. Why do we have social anxiety? How was it ever useful? Why is social anxiety often such a long-term problem even when things don't seem to go wrong? How does anxiety change? How does exposure work to reduce anxiety, and why is it that it sometimes doesn't work? What are the common thinking errors that make us prone to social anxiety, and how can we change them? We often fear that people will think we seem awkward or sound stupid. What will actually happen if we test this out and intentionally act a little odd to see what really happens? How can we gain greater acceptance of ourselves, and what techniques can we use right now to begin that process? How can we learn to accept the sensations we have that accompany our anxiety rather than think we need to eliminate any sensations that are uncomfortable? How can we direct compassion toward ourselves so that our self-criticism is replaced by self-kindness? And what practical social skills can we use so that we do not seem as rigid or as overly cautious as we sometimes do? This superb book not only answers these questions, but also gives you tools you can use to overcome your social anxiety.

When I work with patients, I often think about what it is like for this person coping with their anxiety and depression. Hofmann is insightful, intelligent, and compassionate. This practical book will make you feel that there's somebody by your side while you are reading who understands exactly what you're going through. And you will feel the hope rising in your heart as you discover that there is a way to overcome your social anxiety. You don't have to feel like you have to live up to unrealistic standards, criticize yourself, avoid situations that make you anxious, or even fear your uncomfortable feelings. You can learn to see things more realistically and learn from the exposure that your negative predictions will almost never happen and that, in fact, you are able to cope with negative outcomes even if they do occur. You can learn not only to face your fears but also to develop the confidence to become more resilient.

The good news is that this book, *CBT for Social Anxiety: Proven-Effective Skills to Face Your Fears, Build Confidence, and Enjoy Social Situations*, is an excellent guide to understanding the complexity of social anxiety disorder and learning many proven tools to reverse it.

Building on the most advanced contemporary research on evolutionary theory, neuroscience, behavioral processes, and cognitive behavior therapy, Hofmann walks us through the steps to understand that the avoidance we often use to cope with our anxiety only facilitates and eventually reinforces our negative beliefs.

What I found refreshing in this book is Professor Hofmann's ability to integrate the work from different approaches rather than simply embrace one. In other words, there are several processes at work that underlie social anxiety disorder, and to ignore any one of these processes is to limit the effectiveness of the treatments that one can use.

We live in a culture that seems to emphasize our social performance, giving us unrealistic standards of being completely in control. We are supposed to seem confident, cool, and collected, no matter what. What would happen if we gave up on these demanding standards? Most people know that exposing themselves to the situation that makes them anxious is important in overcoming their fears. But people sometimes say, "I've done those things and I still have this anxiety." This is because, as Hofmann explains, after we have exposed ourselves to anxiety-provoking situations, the *interpretations* we make of our experiences—through rumination and self-criticism—are the main ingredients in maintaining social anxiety.

I suspect that individuals who have been suffering from social anxiety disorder who read this excellent book will feel that Professor Hofmann is looking straight into their minds, seeing the frightening world from their perspective. Like any wise and gifted clinician, Professor Hofmann takes you down that road to your fear and helps you walk past it, empowering you to take back your life. This book will help you on every step of your journey.

—Robert L. Leahy, Ph.D.
Director, American Institute for
Cognitive Therapy
Clinical Professor of Psychology, Department
of Psychiatry, Weill Cornell Medical
College, NewYork-Presbyterian Hospital

Introduction

We all feel socially anxious on occasion. Giving a public speech, meeting new people, dealing with authority figures, being observed by others—these are all common situations that make us feel uncomfortable. All of these situations involve other people, and all of them can trigger a fear of negative evaluation by others. You are not alone. For some of us, these situations are not merely uncomfortable; they are terrifying. We then might come up with excuses to avoid giving the speech, going to parties, meeting authorities, or performing in front of others. And for some of us, this anxiety can be so severe that it interferes with our lives. In these cases, the level of social anxiety might have crossed the threshold to social anxiety disorder (SAD), an officially recognized psychiatric condition (also known as social phobia). The good news, however, is that there are very effective strategies to deal with it. These strategies are described in this book.

This book will describe the reasons for social anxiety in great detail. These reasons are not mere assumptions or opinions. They are based on a lot of research, which I will summarize. But this book is not a scientific textbook. It is written for you, the reader who is struggling with social anxiety and is trying to manage it. In this book, I will translate these evidence-based strategies into concrete strategies that you can apply to manage your social anxiety. It turns out that one highly effective strategy is to expose yourself to these very situations that make you want to avoid them. This seems like a paradox. How should confronting what you fear lessen your fear? There are very good reasons why this works. The natural response to anxiety is avoidance because anxiety is a very unpleasant experience. Confronting it takes courage, and right now you are showing signs of courage. Avoidance and anxiety are closely linked. The short-term positive consequence of avoidance is short-term relief; but the long-term negative consequence is to live a restricted, unsatisfying, or even miserable life. If you continue reading, keep an open mind, and are motivated to overcome your anxiety, you will feel better by the end of this book. Studies have shown that when applying these techniques, three out of four people struggling with social anxiety disorder will experience a dramatic and long-lasting improvement in their problems. This book will help you free yourself from the tyranny of social anxiety, allowing you to live a meaningful and happy life.

Perhaps it is not the first book on the subject you have looked at. In this case, whatever you tried before probably didn't really work that well. This time will be different. Please read on and I'll tell you why.

Social anxiety and extreme shyness are very common. Many social situations cause us discomfort. The fear of public speaking is the most commonly endorsed fear, even more common than the fear of dying. In fact, social anxiety is so common that it appears to be a normal human reaction. It ensures that we stay within the expectations of the group and don't violate social norms. Humans are social animals, and social support is essential for our emotional heath. Throughout our history, individuals have had a greater chance to survive in a group, suggesting that social anxiety is evolutionarily adaptive.

Although very common, social anxiety can become so severe that it goes from just being uncomfortable to significantly interfering with one's life. For example, some very talented people may drop out of college because they can't deal with the demands of social performances, or they may choose careers that are clearly below their abilities and talents simply to avoid these situations. This is the bad news. The good news, however, is that there are effective treatments available for those who suffer from this debilitating disorder.

Over the last decade and a half, my colleagues and I have developed a highly effective psychological treatment approach, based on a great deal of research, for treating social anxiety (Hofmann 2007; Hofmann and Otto 2008). This approach utilizes cognitive behavioral therapy (CBT)—a form of psychotherapy that helps people identify and change negative thinking patterns in order to effect positive changes in behavior and mood—specifically tailored to individuals with SAD. Although many earlier studies have delivered this treatment in a group format, my friend Uli Stangier and his colleagues have shown that an individualized approach for some of these strategies will lead to better outcomes (Stangier et al. 2003). Our scholarly paper (Hofmann 2007) that first described this approach became one of the most highly cited papers in the scientific literature, and it has been found to be one of the most effective psychological treatments for SAD (Hofmann and Otto 2008). Numerous studies evaluating this approach have produced impressive effects, demonstrating a 70%–75% success rate, even in the long term. As a result, our treatment approach has been identified as an "empirically supported treatment" by the American Psychological Association (Society of Clinical Psychology, Division 12 n.d.). This book will describe this approach in such a way that you can use it for yourself.

No two people are alike. You have a unique history and unique weaknesses and strengths. For this reason, there is no *single* approach that will target *all* problems for *all* people in the same way. Some strategies will work very well for some people, and other strategies will work better for others. The one-size-fits-all approach rarely leads to success. Yet, this is the approach that most self-help books pursue. This book is different. You will learn to explore and find the *right* strategy that fits *you* to solve *your* specific problem. Social anxiety is a heterogeneous problem. Some people fear social situations because they are extremely shy, others do so because they view themselves very negatively, while still others have a generally healthy sense of self but experience extreme fear in specific social performance situations. This book acknowledges this heterogeneity and targets your specific issues with the right strategies.

I will begin by describing the nature of social anxiety and fear, where it comes from, and what maintains it. You will then learn techniques to manage your fear and reduce your anxiety. With this base established, you will develop tools to deal with different aspects of your social anxiety. The strategies are related but can also be used as stand-alone strategies. You are the expert of your own problem. Therefore, you are in the best position to deal with it. I advise you to work through the entire book and learn all of the strategies first, and then come back to the ones that worked best for you.

The first chapter describes the problem. It will provide you with important information and facts about social anxiety, its clinical expression, its diagnostic definition (i.e., the criteria many doctors use to determine how severe the problem is), its prevalence (i.e., how common the problem is in the general population), its interference in our lives, and its evolutionary significance and biological meaning. You will learn that social anxiety is a common problem, even a normal one, that is part of what makes us human. Without it, our species would not have survived. But social anxiety can also become a problem and even turn into a mental disorder when it surpasses a critical threshold. It then becomes distressing, interfering, and pervasive. To understand why and when this adaptive feeling can turn into a problem, we need to first identify the various components of social anxiety. Only then can we find ways to address the problem.

Chapter 2 reviews the reasons why social anxiety is maintained despite (or perhaps because of) the fact that we are confronted with so many social situations on a daily basis. These maintaining factors are crucial to understand the recommended strategies to overcome the problem and the differences among people in regard to why their social anxiety is maintained. At its core, the theory behind the interventions I'll describe in this book is that people are apprehensive in social situations in part because they perceive the social standard (i.e., expectations and social goals) as being high. They desire to make a particular impression on others while doubting that they will be able to do so, partly because they are unable to define goals and select specific achievable behavioral strategies to reach these goals. This leads to a further increase in social apprehension and self-focused attention, which triggers a number of closely interrelated cognitive responses (i.e., thoughts and beliefs). Specifically, vulnerable individuals exaggerate the likelihood of social mishaps and the potential social costs involved in social situations. Individuals with SAD assume that they are in danger of behaving in an inept and unacceptable fashion and believe that this will result in disastrous consequences. They further believe that they have little control over their anxiety response in social situations and exaggerate the visibility of their anxiety response to other people. These responses are closely associated with each other and with a tendency to perceive oneself negatively in social situations. The activation of these factors leads to an exacerbation of social anxiety. As a result, the person engages in avoidance and/or safety behaviors, followed by post-event rumination. This cycle feeds on itself, ultimately leading to the maintenance and further exacerbation of the problem. The strategies to target each maintaining factor are described in subsequent chapters.

Chapter 3 introduces the strategy called exposure (i.e., confronting yourself with threatening social situations to test your beliefs) and explains why it is such an important tool for overcoming social anxiety. This important chapter points to avoidance as the primary reason why anxiety is being maintained. This is true for any form of anxiety, but the person with social anxiety is not so much avoiding the situation per se, but rather is avoiding facing fear to its fullest. As a result, avoidance strategies can take on many different forms, some of which can be very subtle behaviors that give us a sense of safety. These safety behaviors are an important reason why social anxiety is such a persistent problem.

In chapter 4, we discuss the nature of anxiety-related thoughts and thinking. The two basic maladaptive thinking styles are *probability overestimation* (exaggerating the likelihood of an unpleasant event occurring) and *catastrophic thinking* (making a much bigger deal out of an unpleasant outcome than it really is). You will learn specific techniques, which I refer to as "thinking tools," to combat these maladaptive thinking styles.

Chapter 5 presents an exercise that I have found to be one of the most effective single strategies for treating social anxiety. In some ways, this exercise, focused on confronting social mishaps, is a culmination and combination of many different strategies. My experience is that once patients embrace it, their social anxiety melts like ice cream in the hot desert sun. It's like opening Aladdin's lamp to finally release the genie, who will never want to go back into the lamp.

Chapter 6 targets one of the core aspects of people with social anxiety, their negative and distorted sense of self as a social object. Using attention-training exercises, you will learn how to modify your self-focused attention, and, through practices called "mirror exposure" and "own voice exposure," you will eventually become more comfortable with the way you are and appear. I also discuss a practice called loving-kindness, or *metta*, meditation to enhance your feelings toward yourself and other people. This is particularly helpful for people who struggle with depression in addition to severe social anxiety.

Chapter 7 describes simple tools to bring down your nervous system's arousal so it doesn't get in the way of using other skills. Here, we discuss *interoceptive habituation exercises* and a relaxation exercise. The term "interoception" refers to the experience and perception of your bodily symptoms, such as your heart racing, shortness of breath, blushing, cold hands, and so on. These symptoms can be quite intense and distressing. Through interoceptive habituation exercises, you learn how these symptoms can become less distressing if they occur in social situations. The term *habituation* here refers to a simple form of learning during which your innate response to a stimulus diminishes with repeated presentations. In the case of interoceptive habituation, you are repeatedly presented with scary bodily experiences (e.g., heart racing), gradually leading to a decrease in anxiety. Alternatively, you may choose to actively decrease your arousal and thereby the intensity of these symptoms through a popular relaxation technique called *progressive muscle relaxation*. I should point out, however, that these techniques should not be used as a way to avoid the feeling of fear in the situation. Rather, they should be used in situations when your bodily symptoms are so strong and distressing that they distract you and interfere with your ability to expose yourself to social situations. Consider them as emergency tools that should be used rarely.

Chapter 8 discusses simple tools to improve your social skills—if needed. Although most people with even extreme social anxiety have adequate or very good social skills, some people do struggle with skills problems. Here, I review *context sensitivity and flexibility* as one of the most important aspects of social interaction to consider. Social skills are always context-specific, meaning the specific skills that are called for depend on the circumstances, culture, and so on. I then review some interactional skills and social performance and speaking skills that can help you deal with various social demands.

This book also includes an appendix, where I provide some critical information about medications for social anxiety. This can help guide you if you have questions about medication. Additionally, on the website for this book (http://www.newharbinger.com/51208), you will find some of the worksheets from this book along with a quiz, followed by the answers, so that you may test yourself to see how much you learned from reading this book. (See the very back of this book for more details.)

The strategies outlined in this book to deal with your social anxiety are highly effective. There is a very good chance that you will see dramatic results in only a few weeks because they are supported by a lot of clinical research and clinical practice. Some of the exercises might seem odd, but please give them a chance and try them out. You don't have much to lose. Only your anxiety that has been holding you back.

—Stefan G. Hofmann, Ph.D.
Boston, MA; Frankfurt, Germany;
Cape Cod, MA; and in between

CHAPTER 1

What Is Social Anxiety?

You are about to speak in front of an audience. You feel your heart racing; you are hot and sweaty. Your hands are cold and clammy. Your mind is racing. Your body is tense. You are feeling the looks from the audience. You feel like a complete loser. It's hell. The scene seems unreal, like a dream.

Does this sound familiar? This is what many people experience when asked to give a speech. Although very common, social anxiety is not restricted to public speeches or other social performance situations. Many people feel similarly at parties or dinner groups or when being introduced to somebody, going out on a date, or talking to people on the telephone. The common feature among all of these situations is that they involve other people. Many other situations can elicit social anxiety, and sometimes the experience is quite different from the ones we just described. These social situations are uncomfortable and distressing for a variety of reasons. You might dislike being the center of attention, being observed by others, having to perform in front of others, or being judged—or feeling like you're being judged—by others.

Nobody likes to be judged negatively, and few enjoy being observed or being the center of attention. Therefore, it's quite normal to sometimes feel some anxiety in social situations. There is nothing to be concerned about. In fact, it would be abnormal if you did not experience some social anxiety sometimes. It is quite normal to feel nervous when giving a speech at work or at a family gathering, or when giving a presentation in high school. Almost everybody is nervous when going on a first date or a job interview. Being anxious in front of people who might evaluate you is quite common. The problem starts when social anxiety is too extreme and when it starts to interfere with your life, as in the case with social anxiety disorder. In this chapter, I will describe many faces of social anxiety and discuss the clinical features of the disorder. I will then provide a brief and understandable review of the research on social anxiety, including its biological and social/cultural foundations. This chapter also includes a brief self-assessment to determine your level of social anxiety.

I will frequently use two terms, "fear" and "anxiety." The difference between these two terms is not always very clear, and they are used interchangeably even by experts. For our purpose, we will define *fear* as the emotional response that you experience when being confronted with a feared situation (such as a social situation). It is the more immediate, involuntary response to the feared situation. *Anxiety*, on the other hand, relates to our feelings and thoughts when anticipating a threatening event and when worrying about and planning for an upcoming social event.

Social Anxiety Is Common

The comedian Jerry Seinfeld once noted that people's number-one fear is public speaking, whereas the number two fear is death. He concluded that if you have to go to a funeral, you might prefer lying in the casket to doing the eulogy! His point is well taken: social anxiety is a very common and even "normal" experience. You might be surprised to learn that even people who are used to the spotlight share the experience of social anxiety. Here are a few examples.

Adele

On April 11, 2011, *Rolling Stone* magazine published an article on Adele, the popular singer-songwriter, who revealed the following:

I have the shakes...I'm scared of audiences...I get shitty scared. One show in Amsterdam, I was so nervous I escaped out the fire exit. I've thrown up a couple of times. Once in Brussels, I projectile-vomited on someone. I just gotta bear it. But I don't like touring. I have anxiety attacks a lot... My nerves don't really settle until I'm offstage.

Donny Osmond

Donny Osmond was the lead singer of the Osmond Brothers in the 1960s. He became a teenage star after a string of early 70s solo hits, and then landed a late 80s comeback hit. In an interview with *People Magazine* (5/17/1999), Osmond revealed:

I'd been a little nervous about every one of my performances all my life, but for as long as I can remember—whether I was onstage or in a business meeting—I knew that if I just got that applause at the end of the first song, a laugh when I made a joke, my nervousness would diminish, though never go away. Sometime around 1994, I began feeling a kind of anxiousness unlike anything I'd ever felt before... Once the fear of embarrassing myself grabbed me, I couldn't get loose. It was as if a bizarre and terrifying unreality had replaced everything that was familiar and safe. In the grip of my wildest fears, I was paralyzed, certain that if I made one wrong move, I would literally die. Even more terrifying, I'd have felt relieved to die. The harder I tried to remember the words, the more elusive they became. The best I could do was not black out, and I got through the show, barely, telling myself repeatedly, Stay conscious, stay conscious. And these attacks of nerves weren't only about performing onstage. I remember being so wound up at the prospect of cohosting Live with Regis and Kathie Lee *that I didn't sleep at all the night before and got nauseous before I went on. Another time, my anxiety was so overwhelming during my audition to play the voice to Hercules in the Disney animated feature, my performance was embarrassing. I started to wonder if I could continue a singing career at all.*

Barbara Streisand

Barbara Streisand, American actress, singer, and filmmaker, avoided live performances for nearly three decades due to a debilitating bout of stage fright during a concert in New York's Central Park in 1967, during which she forgot the lyrics to one of her songs. She told Diane Sawyer during an interview (9/22/2005):

I couldn't come out of it… It was shocking to me to forget the words. So, I didn't have any sense of humor about it… You know, I didn't make up words…some performers really do well when they forget the words. They forget the words all the time, but they somehow have humor about it. I remember I didn't have a sense of humor about it. I was quite shocked… I didn't sing and charge people for 27 years because of that night… I was like, "God, I don't know. What if I forget the words again?"

These are just some notable examples of current and past celebrities. Other examples are the singer Carly Simon and many professional athletes, such as baseball players Steve Sax, Mike Ivie, and Steve Blass (for our American sports enthusiasts). The point here is: even people who make a successful living by being at the center of the public eye and performing in front of thousands of people can experience crippling social anxiety. It is extremely common and even affects people who have to deal with social performances on a daily basis.

About 13 out of 100 people in the US are currently struggling or have previously struggled with social anxiety disorder (SAD). This number, known as the lifetime prevalence rate, is somewhat dependent on culture. Within the US, we find higher rates of SAD in American Indians and lower rates in people of Asian, Latino, African American, and Afro-Caribbean descent compared with non-Hispanic Whites. The prevalence rates in children and adolescents are comparable to those in adults, but it seems to decrease with age. Slightly higher rates are seen in females than in males. Members of the LGBTQ+ community are also more likely to suffer from SAD than heterosexual and cisgender people (the latter referring to people whose gender identity corresponds with their sex assigned at birth).

Let's take a look at some people who are not in the public eye. I could fill many volumes with examples. No two people struggling with social anxiety are alike. Each person has a unique story that is colored in unique ways by their social anxiety. The cases I describe here are imagined and composite cases. There is no such thing as a typical person with SAD. But despite these unique differences, all people share the struggle, the distress, and the impairment that this problem can cause in their lives.

Sarah

Sarah, age thirty-three, is not a celebrity. She has never won any major awards in her life. But if she had won them, she would probably have avoided the acceptance speeches because she is terrified of giving public speeches. Her public speaking anxiety has always been a major problem for her. She lives with her husband and two young daughters, ages six and eight, in a middle-class, single-family home. Sarah has worked as a homemaker since the birth of her children, but in the last two years she has returned to outside employment as a paralegal assistant in a law firm.

Sarah has been socially anxious since grade school. She reports that her time alone with her children was a respite from the worst of her social anxiety, but now that she has returned to a work setting, she realizes that she finally needs to attend to her social anxiety. In seeking treatment, she stated that she needs to be less anxious at work and at social gatherings, but that she also wants to be less anxious so that she provides a better role model for her children.

Sarah is warm and supportive. She is happily married to Carl, a bus driver. They have been married for more than ten years and live a "pretty good" life. Her biggest problem is her "lifelong social anxiety disorder." Sarah described herself as being "socially utterly incompetent" and a "total social loser." She stated that when confronted with certain social evaluative situations, such as public speeches, she feels panicky. She describes this feeling as a state of strong bodily symptoms characterized by heart racing, being flushed, trembling, and dry mouth. She stated that the only way to stop these symptoms is by leaving the situation.

She feels a great deal of sadness and frustration because she had a number of "missed opportunities"—for example, she turned down several attractive job offers—as a result of her social anxiety. At the same time, Sarah very often avoids social situations because she fears being humiliated and embarrassed. If she cannot avoid them, she endures them with extreme distress and tends to ruminate about them long after the event has passed. One of her worst situations is going to Parent-Teacher Association (PTA) meetings at her daughters' school. She wants to serve as a good model to her children and give them the best chances for a good education. She fears that she comes across as stupid and incompetent and is concerned that people judge her negatively, which will ultimately affect her children's education.

Joseph

Joseph, age twenty-five, is seeking help for his debilitating, pervasive, and lifelong social anxiety. Joseph avoids any social contact with other people and even feels restraint when interacting with his parents and other relatives. He desires companionship but is unwilling to get involved with people because he is preoccupied with being criticized or rejected. He still lives in his parents' home, where he grew up. He feels trapped and isolated and wishes he could have a job and a relationship and lead a "normal" life.

Joseph dropped out of high school in ninth grade when he was asked to give a presentation in front of his class. To avoid this assignment, he ran away from home and spent the night on the street. When the police found him the next day, his parents started homeschooling him. Since that time, Joseph has never returned to school or to see any of his classmates again. Although his family has been very supportive and understanding, he also finds the relationship with them to be very difficult. Both of his parents were born and raised in Germany and immigrated to the United States in their thirties. He described his father as very strict, domineering, authoritarian, and overinvolved, and his mother as submissive and conflict-avoidant. Joseph has two older sisters. He considers the younger of the two to be his best friend. He speaks to her once a week for a few minutes on the phone. In addition to having social anxiety, Joseph also feels very depressed and worries excessively about various minor matters. Although his attractiveness is above average, he sees himself as physically unappealing, socially inept, and inferior to others. Because of his problems, he has occasional thoughts about suicide but has denied any intent or plan to harm himself.

Carrie

Carrie is a fifty-year-old single, nonbinary postal worker who uses the pronoun they. They have always been very shy. Carrie feels inadequate and depressed. They cannot remember ever feeling comfortable in social situations. Even in grade school, their mind would go blank when they had to speak in front of a group of people. They avoided going to birthday parties and other social gatherings when they could, or, if they had to attend, they would just sit there quietly. In school, they were very quiet and would only answer questions in class when they wrote down the answers in advance. But even then, they would frequently mumble or not be able to get the answer out clearly. When meeting new children, they kept their eyes lowered, fearing the children would make fun of them.

As Carrie grew older, they had a few playmates in their neighborhood, but they never really had a "best" friend. Their school grades were fairly good, except in subjects that required classroom participation. As a teenager, they were especially anxious in informal interactions with other classmates. Although Carrie would like to have a relationship, they have never gone on a date or asked another person out because of a fear of rejection. Carrie attended college and did well for a while. But when they were expected to give oral presentations in class, Carrie stopped attending class and eventually dropped out. For a few years after that, they had trouble finding a job because they didn't think they were capable of going on job interviews. Eventually, they found some jobs for which only a written test was required. A number of years ago, Carrie was offered, and accepted, a job in the post office to work the evening shift. They were offered several promotions, but Carrie refused them because they feared the social pressures. Carrie has a number of acquaintances at work, but no real friends, and avoids all invitations to socialize with coworkers after their shifts.

Carrie is terrified of most social situations and avoids them as much as possible. If they can't avoid them, they overprepare and often develop scripts beforehand so they know what to say. But despite this, Carrie feels extreme fear when confronted with social situations. They often monitor and observe themself in social situations and are often disgusted by their own incompetence. They simply do not think they have what it takes to handle social situations. Carrie often feels overwhelming anxiety marked by strong physiological sensations, such as a racing heart, sweaty palms, and trembling. They have been trying to control their anxiety in social situations with a medication called propranolol, a beta-blocker. This has been fairly ineffective, so recently their doctor advised them to try paroxetine. However, they do not like the idea of taking medication.

Like Sarah, Joseph, Carrie, and even celebrities such as Adele, Donny Osmond, and Barbara Streisand, most of us know what it's like to feel anxious and fearful in social situations. But when does it go from common-place problem to mental health disorder? This is a complicated question, particularly for something as common as social anxiety. One important feature that distinguishes anxiety as an unpleasant experience from a disor-der is how much it interferes with the person's life. Despite their anxiety, Adele, Donny Osmond, and Barbara Streisand are able to function quite well in public. But for others, like Sarah, the level of social anxiety in these situations can be so high that it causes significant distress and interference in their lives. These people often make important life choices that are at least partly based on their social anxiety. As a result, they may choose a career that requires fewer social situations; they may turn down a promo-tion to avoid formal speaking; they may remain single or marry just to avoid dating situations; or they may live very isolated lives with very few friends.

So one important feature that distinguishes normal from abnormal anxiety is the level of subjective distress and impact it has on the person's life. Shortly we will take a closer look at how to determine when social anxiety is "normal" and when it is excessive. We will then look at the reasons why social anxiety is so persistent, going over concrete strategies for targeting those reasons specifically. First, though, let's explore some of the evolutionary and scientific findings regarding social anxiety.

Why Social Anxiety?

Being a little shy and introverted is not a problem. To the contrary. Many well-known politicians and perhaps even some of your friends and coworkers could use a little introversion. Having some social anxiety might even be desirable. We seem sensitive to anger, criticism, or other means of social disapproval and have a natural desire to belong and be accepted by our peers. Early signs of social anxiety are present in the typical development of humans. For example, between eight and nine months after birth, humans show signs of anxiety in front of strangers. This development coincides with the growing attachment to the mother (or whoever is the primary caregiver). In other words, almost all of us have been socially anxious at least one time or another.

So it seems that some degree of social anxiety is necessary and adaptive. Evolutionary pressure encourages social cooperation. Groups are much more likely to survive than single individuals without the support of a group. Groups enable humans to conquer incredible challenges. Groups enable the delegation of responsibilities. In hunter-gatherer societies, children are raised by mothers while fathers collect food and occasionally hunt for prey that could not be captured alone. Similarly, a pack of wolves is considerably more successful at hunting than a single animal. Groups provide the necessary social structure to form a meta-organism—the beehive, the flock of birds, the school of fish, and the tribes and cultural groups of humans. Being part of a group, therefore, is an evolutionary necessity of survival. Social psychologists have called this *the need to belong*.

The British researchers Peter Trower and Paul Gilbert assume that the evolutionary purpose of social anxiety might be to facilitate the functioning of complex social groups, thereby increasing the likelihood of survival for each individual member and the human species as a whole (Trower and Gilbert 1989). According to this theory, access to resources, such as food, sexual partners, personal space, and so forth, is associated with a higher position in the social hierarchy. Therefore, group members either compete for a higher rank in the group hierarchy or at least attempt to maintain their current rank. According to this theory, such a situation would lead to constant and bitter battles between group members, which could eventually jeopardize the survival of the entire group, unless there was a regulatory system in place to counteract this tendency.

Trower and Gilbert assume that the subordinate members' social anxiety toward the dominating members of the group and willingness to signal submission constitutes such a regulatory system because it prevents or limits conflict between group members. But what might have been true during the early phase of human evolution might not be true today. The function of a trait, even if it had one, might have changed over the millennia. Still, it's possible that at one point, social anxiety might have had an important evolutionary survival value, perhaps because it motivated submissive behaviors in subordinate members and inhibited aggressive behaviors from the dominant members, which might have allowed the subordinate members to remain part of the social group and in proximity of the dominant members. Thus, social anxiety may be the manifestation of the instinct for self-preservation. But, again, what was helpful back then is, in modern society, annoying at the least and disabling at the worst. If social fears interfere with our lives, they can then become problematic and maladaptive. Later research has shown some support for Trower and Gilbert's model and further suggests that individuals with SAD perceive social threats as challenges to social bonds and to their relative standing in the social hierarchy (Gilboa-Schectman et al. 2014; Johnson et al. 2021).

Eye contact seems to occupy a special role in human social interactions. It is perhaps the most basic form of social contact between humans. The Swedish researchers Arne Öhman, Ulf Dimberg, and their colleagues believe that some social fears are the result of a biologically determined "readiness" to easily associate fear with angry, critical, or rejecting faces (Öhman 1986). In fact, angry faces and happy faces lead to a different pattern of physiological arousal—as indicated by electrodermal activity (i.e., electrical activity in the skin)—even in non-anxious people (Dimberg and Öhman 1983; Dimberg et al., 2000). People can "learn" how to fear faces by pairing a picture of a face with an unpleasant stimulus (such as a light electric shock). The type of learning that occurs under these circumstances is referred to as "conditioning." In a typical conditioning experiment by Öhman and his colleagues, participants see pictures of happy, angry, and neutral faces followed by a slight but unpleasant electric shock. This leads to an increase in electrodermal activity, which is the result of subtle changes in the skin's sweat glands. The researchers found that after a few trials (i.e., paired presentations) of the faces and the electrical shock, the presentation of the faces alone would elicit the same electrodermal response as the electric shock. The type of learning that has occurred is known in psychology as "classical conditioning," which is one of the most primitive learning mechanisms. If the pictures are repeatedly presented without the shock, the electrodermal response eventually becomes weaker. This type of unlearning is called "extinction."

Interestingly, people show much more resistance to extinction to angry faces than to neutral or happy faces (Dimberg and Öhman 1983). It appears that for some reason, Mother Nature allows us to forget neutral or happy faces, but she does not want us to forget angry faces, perhaps because remembering an angry face gives us an evolutionary advantage by avoiding harm in the future. This effect is only seen if the person on the picture looks directly at the subject. Angry faces looking away are as ineffective as happy faces in conditioning paradigms (Dimberg and Öhman 1983). Thus, direct eye contact seems to be crucial. Some species, such as certain butterflies, use patterns that resemble large staring eyes to protect themselves from predators. In other species, such as our close relatives, the primates, direct eye contact also seems to be very frightening. Avoiding eye contact, on the other hand, is a sign of submissiveness and fear. In humans, the response to eye contact is obviously greatly altered by contextual and learning factors, but it seems to be there nevertheless.

So what does all this have to do with social anxiety? Isaac Marks, a psychiatrist at the Maudsley institute in London and one of the first scientists who studied SAD, suggested that the fear of being watched among individuals with social phobia (now called social anxiety disorder) is an exaggeration of the normal human sensitivity to eyes (Marks 1987). In fact, it was shown that vigilance to the eye region of faces, especially angry faces, is characteristic of adolescents with SAD. Adolescents with SAD seem more drawn to the eye region than teens without SAD (Capriola-Hall et al. 2021).

Eye contact in humans, however, is not exclusively associated with anger and dominance. It is also associated with affection and compassion. The common element seems to be closeness and reduction of personal space. Individuals who do not want to give up or decrease their personal space will perceive eye contact as threatening and uncomfortable. In fact, individuals with extreme social anxiety sometimes even avoid their own eye contact when looking at themselves in the mirror. This could be explained in part by a generalization effect of the sensitivity to eyes (i.e., any two dark circles next to each other resembling two eyes looking at you may cause some discomfort). In addition, we know that mirror exposure leads to an increase in self-focused attention, which is uncomfortable to many socially anxious people. Combined with negative self-perception and self-criticism, mirror exposure can therefore lead to heightened anxiety in some people with SAD (Hofmann and Heinrichs 2003). We will revisit this again at a later point.

When Social Anxiety Becomes a Problem

Homo sapiens are social animals. We accomplish incredible feats that no other animal is able to do because of the social structures we are able to create. We have a strong desire to form such social structures. We cluster in cities and want to be with others. Because of our close social contacts, we are still struggling to contain COVID-19 as I am writing these words. At the same time, our social structure and culture has created the science that will probably free us eventually from the tyranny of this virus. None of this would have been possible without the support we provide each other. Whenever social anxiety limits your social support, it can become a problem, and a serious one, too. Social support exists when at least two individuals can exchange resources with the intention that the provider of this support enhances the well-being of the recipient. Loneliness—the absence of such social support—is one of the greatest risk factors for all different problems, ranging from heart disease to suicide. Social anxiety can become a problem if it prevents us from utilizing our social support system that we rely on. For our mental health, this social support system enables us to effectively regulate our emotions.

Emotion regulation, our ability to control our emotional state, is a fundamental aspect of human socialization. We learn as children to respond to social situations based on other people's inner states rather than to their outward behaviors, and we learn to consider ourselves in relation to our past version of ourselves and to anticipate the future version of ourselves. This process is largely influenced by how our caregivers react, verbally and nonverbally, to our emotions and by how they express and discuss emotions. Later in life, emotion regulation receives increasing influence through our peer context. As adults, our relationships often mirror the infant-caregiver bond, meaning that we respond negatively to social isolation and positively to social bonding and affiliation. These interpersonal factors are essential in emotion regulation, because emotion regulation develops within a social context and continues to include social relations throughout life (Hofmann 2014; Hofmann and Doan 2018). There appear to be at least four different ways that we regulate emotions through others (Hofmann et al. 2016): (1) by enhancing our positive affect (we seek out others to increase feelings of happiness and joy), (2) through perspective taking (we consider others' situations to be reminded not to worry and that others have it worse), (3) for soothing (we seek out others for comfort and sympathy), and (4) through social modeling (we look to others to see how they might cope with a given situation). Social anxiety can restrict us in the use of these important interpersonal emotion regulation strategies, reducing support and leading to social isolation and loneliness.

When Social Anxiety Becomes a Disorder

The defining feature of social anxiety disorder is the excessive fear of negative evaluation by other people. This often happens when we are the center of attention and when we are asked to perform in front of others. We are constantly exposed to other people, often stand in the center of attention, and frequently have to perform in front of others. We all have experienced important test situations in front of others, such as oral exams and public speeches. But even on a daily basis we are confronted with such situations, only on a small scale. For example, we may need to sign something in front of people or count change in front of people or give people directions or ask for directions, and so on.

Social anxiety disorder was first recognized as a psychiatric condition only in 1980 with the publication of the third edition of the *Diagnostic and Statistical Manual of Mental Disorders* (DSM-III), published by the American Psychiatric Association (APA 1980). The goal of the DSM is to define and describe all known psychiatric conditions (i.e., mental disorders), one of which is social anxiety disorder (SAD).

The DSM defines psychological disorders by listing a set of criteria that identify the most important features of the disorder. The most recent revision of these criteria was published in 2005 in its fifth edition, the DSM-5 (APA 2013). The World Health Organization also publishes a diagnostic manual, currently in its eleventh revision, called the *International Classification of Mental Disorders* (ICD-11). The ICD-11 criteria for SAD are very similar to those in the DSM-5.

Following are the diagnostic criteria for SAD listed in the ICD-11 (*International Classification of Diseases*, Eleventh Revision [ICD-11], World Health Organization [WHO] 2019/2021 https://icd.who.int/browse11).

Essential (Required) Features

- Marked and excessive fear or anxiety that occurs consistently in one or more social situations such as social interactions (e.g., having a conversation), doing something while feeling observed (e.g., eating or drinking in the presence of others), or performing in front of others (e.g., giving a speech).

- The individual is concerned that he or she will act in a way, or show anxiety symptoms, that will be negatively evaluated by others (i.e., be humiliating, embarrassing, lead to rejection, or be offensive).

- Relevant social situations are consistently avoided or endured with intense fear or anxiety.

- The symptoms are not transient; that is, they persist for an extended period of time (e.g., at least several months).

- The symptoms are not better accounted for by another mental disorder (e.g., Agoraphobia, Body Dysmorphic Disorder, Olfactory Reference Disorder).

- The symptoms result in significant distress about experiencing persistent anxiety symptoms or significant impairment in personal, family, social, educational, occupational, or other important areas of functioning. If functioning is maintained, it is only through significant additional effort.

The defining feature is a marked and excessive fear or anxiety in one or more social situations. Some people with SAD are only afraid of certain performance situations (such as public speaking, eating in a restaurant, using a public lavatory, or writing while people are watching), while others show a broad array of fears that may include numerous social and interactional situations (such as meeting new people, going out on a date, or saying no to unreasonable requests). Some people report concerns about physical symptoms, such as blushing, sweating, or trembling, rather than initially endorsing fears of negative evaluation.

Children often undergo periods of social anxiety. Stranger anxiety, for example, is a very typical developmental milestone. Therefore, it is important not to pathologize normal behaviors. People with SAD fear that they act in a way or show anxiety symptoms that will be negatively evaluated by others, invariably causing intense anxiety. They then avoid certain, or numerous, social situations or endure them under great distress. As noted before, social anxiety is very common. Therefore, the degree of anxiety should be considered in relation to societal and cultural norms. Still, this anxiety is not considered a clinical issue unless it causes significant distress or impairment in the person's life, is not attributable to the effects of a substance or another medical condition, and lasts for at least six months. Thus, the bar to meet a diagnosis of SAD if fairly high because if social anxiety is caused by other problems, SAD cannot be assigned.

The bottom line is that social anxiety is only a (diagnosable) problem if one or more social situations almost always cause extreme anxiety that is excessive, persistent, and distressing or interferes with your life. It is obviously very subjective and culturally dependent whether social anxiety is in fact "excessive" and "interfering," and this ultimately depends on your own definition.

When social anxiety crosses the threshold to a clinical diagnosis, it often becomes a very debilitating and interfering problem. Some people live isolated and lonely lives, others choose careers that are far below their capabilities in order to avoid social contact, others take prescribed medication in order to feel comfortable in social situations, and still others become dependent on drugs or alcohol as a result of their social anxiety. Research studies have confirmed this. One of the earliest studies suggesting that SAD is a serious problem was conducted by Frank Schneier, the late Michael Liebowitz, and colleagues from Columbia University. The authors interviewed thirty-two people with SAD to examine the degree of interference of SAD on people's lives (Schneier et al. 1994). This group was compared to fourteen individuals who did not receive the diagnosis of SAD. The results showed that individuals with SAD were rated as more impaired than those without SAD on nearly all areas in their lives, including education, employment, family, romantic relationships, and friendships. More than half of the people with SAD reported at least moderate impairment at some point in their lives. More recent studies (e.g., Stein et al. 2000; Wong et al. 2012) found very similar results, even showing that the more social fears a person had, the greater their impairment (Stein et al. 2000).

In an earlier study, Murray Stein and his Canadian colleagues examined more specifically the impact of public speaking anxiety on people's lives (Stein et al. 1996). The authors wanted to examine whether this very common problem had any notable effect on people lives. The authors randomly called up 499 residents of Winnipeg, Manitoba (a pretty nippy place up in Canada), and asked them whether they experience excessive fear when asked to speak in front of a large audience. As many as one third of all respondents reported that they did suffer from excessive public speaking anxiety. Further questioning revealed that most of these people (90%) had developed this anxiety by the age of twenty. In total, 49 of the 499 people who were interviewed (10%) reported that public speaking anxiety had caused them marked distress or had resulted in marked interference with work, social life, or education. Interestingly, public speaking anxiety in isolation (i.e., without any other social fears) is not very common. Only twenty-three people reported anxiety only in public speaking situations (5%). This is a consistent finding in the literature: social anxiety is rarely limited to only one situation, such as public speaking, and those performance situations lead to significant distress and interference with the person's life.

Social Anxiety Is Pervasive

Once a problem is defined, the next question we need to ask is how common the problem is. Researchers were surprised about how common the problem was. Epidemiological studies (i.e., studies that examine how common psychiatric conditions are in the general population) showed that the lifetime prevalence rate of SAD in Western cultures is around 13% of the population. This means that about 13 in 100 people meet or have met the criteria for this disorder at one point in their lives. These data were largely based on the work of Ronald Kessler, an epidemiologist at Harvard University, and his colleagues. In one study, his team interviewed more than 8,000 people between the ages of 15 and 54 living in 172 counties in 34 states in the US (Kessler et al. 1994). The results showed that 13.3% of Americans met the DSM diagnostic criteria for SAD at least at one point in their lives and 8% met those criteria within the last year of the interview, making SAD the third most common mental disorder in the US population, with slightly more women than men meeting diagnostic criteria. Only depression and alcohol problems are more common. SAD is often associated with depression as well as alcohol and drug abuse, possibly because people get depressed because of SAD and use alcohol or drugs to feel more comfortable in social situations. However, not all people with social anxiety are depressed or use alcohol or drugs. In fact, less than one third of individuals with SAD develop such problems.

Whether you meet the criteria for SAD can only be determined by a thorough diagnostic interview by a mental health care professional. But let's take a look at how you compare to others. Please rate your fear on a scale from 0 (not at all) to 10 (very much) for the following six social situations:

1. having a first date

2. using the telephone

3. being introduced to people

4. meeting people in authority

5. being teased

6. being under observation by others

If you rated four or more of those six situations as 4 or higher, your social anxiety is likely to be of a generalized subtype (which is the case in almost 30%–50% of all people with SAD). The generalized subtype of SAD was a diagnostic subtype in earlier editions of the DSM. Although this subtype category is no longer part of the DSM-5, it is still a good marker of social anxiety severity. If you do not rate four or more of these situations with 4 or higher on a 0–10-point scale, your social anxiety is either less extreme or limited to only a certain type of social situation, such as public speaking. In this case, it is still possible that you meet criteria for SAD.

In order to determine which situations are the most fear-provoking ones for you personally, it is often useful to establish a "fear and avoidance hierarchy." This lists the ten most fear-provoking situations in a hierarchy with rank #1 being the most fear provoking, rank #2 being the second most fear-provoking, and so forth, along with ratings for your level of fear and level of avoidance.

Let's illustrate this with a concrete example of such a hierarchy. Let's take Sarah. Her most fear-provoking situation is giving a speech at her PTA meeting. Although she is very afraid of this situation (she gave it a rating of

100 on a scale of 0–100), she can't always avoid it (she rated her avoidance as 90). Even attending the meeting, her second-highest ranking, is very anxiety producing (80). When looking more closely at the various situations she listed, it becomes clear that they all have to do with formal or informal social interactions or presentations. Here is her fear and avoidance hierarchy.

Table 1: Sarah's Fear and Avoidance Hierarchy

Social Situation	Fear (0–100)	Avoidance (0–100)
My worst fear: Expressing my opinion at a PTA meeting	100	90
My 2nd worst fear: Attending the PTA meeting	80	80
My 3rd worst fear: Talking to a teacher	80	80
My 4th worst fear: Sitting at a big conference table discussing things	80	60
My 5th worst fear: Giving a presentation to our trainees	80	60
My 6th worst fear: Talking to coworkers	70	70
My 7th worst fear: Introducing myself to new coworkers	70	20
My 8th worst fear: Going to a party	50	60
My 9th worst fear: Leading a conference call	50	10
My 10th worst fear: Assigning unpleasant tasks to trainees	30	10

What is your personal fear and avoidance hierarchy? Knowing this can help with the intervention plan we will be discussing later on. Please go ahead and generate your own personal Fear and Avoidance Hierarchy. You can download a blank table from the website for this book, http://www.newharbinger.com/51208.

The Multiple Faces of Social Anxiety

Let's take a closer look at how social anxiety is expressed. Joseph and Carrie fear virtually all social situations and have been avoiding them all their lives. Sarah's most feared situation is giving a presentation at her Wednesday morning meetings. I am sure you can relate to this. Imagine that you have to give an important speech in front of a really big audience. If you couldn't avoid the situation altogether or take any medication or alcohol to reduce your level of anxiety, what would you typically experience?

Anxiety is expressed in three different ways (see figure 1), namely in the form of thoughts (what we think), bodily symptoms (what we feel), and behaviors (how we act). For example, if I forced you to give an impromptu speech in front of strangers, you might be experiencing intense fear and anxiety. Your heart might be racing and your hands may be getting cold (your bodily symptoms), you might think *I will embarrass myself* and *People will think I am stupid* (your thoughts), and you might tighten up and try to get out of the situation (your behaviors).

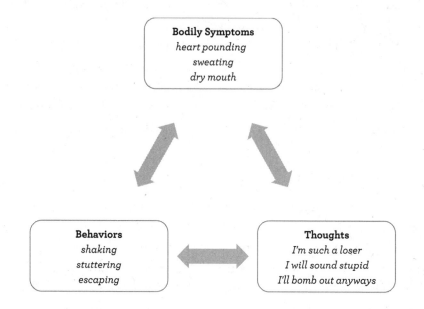

Figure 1: The Three Components of Social Anxiety (copyright Stefan G. Hofmann, 2022)

If you are faced with a potentially threatening situation (e.g., having to speak publicly), you may experience a number of physiological sensations (e.g., shaking). Consequently, you will likely have a negative cognition, or thought, predicting failure or danger (e.g., *I'm such a loser*), which, in turn, will only serve to heighten your physiological levels of arousal. As these physical sensations increase, you will likely be less able to focus upon the task at hand. And instead of alleviating your anxiety with coping statements (e.g., *If I forget my place, I can always look at my note cards*), your maladaptive cognitions will become more intense (e.g., *If I stumble, everyone will think that I'm stupid and unprepared*). The end result will likely be extreme levels of anxiety as well as poor performance or avoidance of the anxiety-provoking situation (e.g., *I'll just call in sick the day of my presentation*).

This is a maladaptive response to the threat. There are alternative, more adaptive ways of responding. For example, once you first notice the physical symptoms of anxiety, you can practice more rational responses (e.g., *Everyone gets nervous before these presentations*) to prevent an exacerbation of these physical symptoms. With continued encouraging statements to yourself, or self-talk (e.g., *I can make a few mistakes and the talk can still go well*), your anxiety levels will remain at a reasonable level. As a result, your functioning will likely not be disrupted and the outcome will be successful. And, given the sense of mastery that will result from this experience, you are more likely to have more adaptive responses in the future. Let's zoom in on these aspects of fear: the bodily component, the thoughts, and the behaviors.

The Bodily Component

The bodily component of extreme fear is seen in the form of panic attacks. A panic attack is a brief episode of extreme fear. Sometimes, these episodes come out of the blue and for no apparent reason (as in panic disorder); sometimes they are linked to specific objects or situations, such as when talking to a stranger or giving a speech. Therefore, panic attacks can also play an important role in social anxiety, as is true for other states of fear and acute anxiety. A panic attack typically lasts for a few minutes and is associated with intense bodily sensations, such as heart pounding, dizziness, shortness of breath, sweating, shaking, tingling in the hands and feet, chest pain, nausea, a feeling of choking, and feelings of unreality. As already noted, panic attacks can happen in many different situations. They are often triggered by—or are more likely to occur in—a certain situation (such as a social situation). At other times, the attacks can come on completely unexpectedly. Panic attacks are closely associated with what we call the *fight-or-flight response system*. They are the expression of an innate alarm system that Mother Nature provided us with, which used to serve an important survival role. Typically, this alarm system goes off when we are confronted with real danger. These are the "true alarms." The inherent danger in social situations is not a threat to our life, but rather to our status in the social hierarchy. We may perceive a social situation as dangerous if it threatens our standing in the social hierarchy, which affects our self-worth, self-esteem, and self-confidence.

As with your smoke alarm at home, our alarm system for social threat can also go off even though there is no real danger present. These attacks are called "false alarms." As you know, false alarms can happen for a number of different reasons. Cooking, smoking a cigar, or the steam coming out of a hot shower can set off the smoke alarm, although there is no real danger (i.e., fire) present. Similarly, our innate alarm system can be set off by a number of different things that do not constitute real danger to us. It is enough if we *believe* that we are in danger to set off the alarm. Because we often have to perform in social situations, such false alarms can distract us from the task at hand and disrupt our performance, leading us to then perceive performance situations as an even greater threat.

The Cognitive Component

Thoughts (also known as cognitions) associated with feared situations are typically quite specific to the nature of the particular situation. Let's continue with Sarah's most feared situation: public speaking. Public speaking is, in fact, the most commonly feared social situation. To see how you compare to most other people in this specific social situation, my colleague Patricia DiBartolo and I have developed and tested a brief and useful instrument, the Self-Statements during Public Speaking (SSPS) scale, to measure an important aspect of your public speaking anxiety: your thoughts related to public speaking (Hofmann and DiBartolo 2000). Research has shown that people with SAD have a lot of negative thoughts and only a few positive thoughts when thinking about social situations. Let's see how you compare to other people in your thoughts related to public speaking by following these steps:

Step 1: Please imagine what you have typically felt and thought to yourself during any kind of public speaking situation. Imagining these situations, how much do you agree with the statements below? Please rate the degree of your agreement on a scale from 0 (do not agree at all) to 5 (agree completely). Write the number corresponding to each item in a notebook or your smartphone.

1. What do I have to lose? It's worth a try.

2. I'm a loser.

3. This is an awkward situation but I can handle it.

4. A failure in this situation would be more proof of my incapacity.

5. Even if things don't go well, it's no catastrophe.

6. I can handle everything.

7. What I say will probably sound stupid.

8. I'll probably "bomb out" anyway.

9. Instead of worrying I could concentrate on what I want to say.

10. I feel awkward and dumb; they're bound to notice.

Step 2: Now add together your ratings for items 1, 3, 5, 6, and 9. This is your score of the "Positive Self-Statement Scale" (SSPS-P). And now add together your ratings for items 2, 4, 7, 8, and 10. This is your score on the "Negative Self-Statement Scale" (SSPS-N). As a reference point, college students have an average SSPS-P score between 15 and 16 and an average SSPS-N score between 7 and 8. In contrast, people with SAD score, on average, two points lower on the SSPS-P (between 13 and 14) and slightly above 12 on the SSPS-N.

Obviously, you could be suffering from SAD even if your score is higher than 16 on the SSPS-P and lower than 7 on the SSPS-N. Approximately 70% of people with SAD who are anxious in public speaking situations score between 7 and 19 on the SSPS-P and between 6 and 18 on the SSPS-N. In contrast, approximately 70% of college students have SSPS-P scores between 11 and 20 and SSPS-N scores between 2 and 12. This shows that the distribution of scores between anxious and non-anxious people overlaps. In other words, it is certainly possible that you suffer from SAD but show lower SSPS-N and higher SSPS-P scores than some non-anxious students. However, on average, people with SAD score higher on the SSPS-N and lower on the SSPS-P scale than non-anxious people. High scores on the SSPS-N in particular suggest that your public speaking anxiety is atypically high. For example, if your SSPS-P score is 15.5 and your SSPS-N score is 7.5, you are well within the norms of a college population. In contrast, if your scores on the SSPS-P and SSPS-N are 13.5 and 12.5, you are well within the population of people with SAD.

The Behavioral Component

Escape—the flight aspect of the fight-or-flight response system—seems to be the most natural and effective response to eliminate suffering. However, social conventions and negative social sanctions often make it very difficult to escape a situation. Therefore, people use other behaviors to reduce or eliminate anxiety. The most effective one next to escape is probably avoidance (not entering the situation in the first place). Other behaviors may include taking anti-anxiety medication and drinking alcohol or tea before the event. None of these behaviors are helpful. Ever. Some anxious performers attempt to reduce their anxiety by distracting themselves, repeatedly thinking about a certain phrase or song, imagining being somewhere else, or picturing the audience without any clothes. Many of these so-called "coping strategies" are recommended in other books on public speaking anxiety. Other performers go through bizarre superstitious rituals in an attempt to reduce their anxiety before or during social situations. In some cases, these rituals are even publicly displayed and publicly reinforced, as often displayed by professional athletes.

People do these things in order to feel some control over a seemingly uncontrollable situation, which makes the situation less uncomfortable. To put it another way, the purpose of these behaviors is to avoid the feeling of anxiety in social situations. Therefore, all of these behaviors (rituals, taking medication or alcohol, distracting yourself, ending a speech prematurely and walking away, or not entering the situation in the first place) lead to avoidance of fear. For the remainder of this book I will therefore define avoidance broadly as *anything that you do or don't do that prevents you from facing your fear.* Please note that this definition is not just restricted to refusing to enter a feared situation. The definition also includes escaping from the feared situation, taking medications, distracting yourself, using breathing techniques…*anything* that prevents you from facing your fear.

The three components of social anxiety (thoughts, behavior, and bodily symptoms) are closely connected through a positive feedback loop, which can easily spiral into a panic attack. Let's assume, for example, that your boss comes into your office and asks you to give a presentation about something that you are not very familiar with in front of a large group of people in a few minutes. You may think, *There is no way on earth that I can do this; I will humiliate myself* (cognitive component). You may feel your heart rate racing and your muscles becoming tense (bodily component). You may also think, *I am so nervous. I know I will mess up the situation; I can't do this* (cognitive component again). You may then check your watch every few seconds and start pacing in your office (behavioral component), you may then think again, *There is really no way I can do this* (cognitive component), you may feel sweaty and hot (bodily component), and you may finally give your boss an excuse as to why you can't give this presentation right now (behavioral component). This example illustrates how the different components of anxiety interact and feed into each other.

Scientists often refer to this fear reaction as the fight-or-flight response. The fear reaction is conceptualized as an alarm system that is activated if we perceive a situation as being threatening and unsafe. Mother Nature gave us this response system because it increases our chance of survival in the wild. However, the cultural development of humans turned some evolutionarily adaptive behaviors into rather annoying rudiments of ancient times. For example, many people are afraid of snakes, spiders, and other animals that are potentially threatening in the wilderness but are of no real threat in modern civilization. In contrast, evolution did not provide us with an alarm system that protects us from real danger in our current world, such as touching electric outlets or drinking bleach. In other words, some fears, and in particular those that were evolutionarily adaptive, are more common and are more easily acquired than others. Apparently, evolution prepared us to acquire certain fears—including social ones—but not others. And, certainly, not all of us have acquired, or maintained, such fears.

So Why Me?

There is no easy answer to this question, and different people develop social anxiety for different reasons. Some people have been shy all their lives and feel uncomfortable in any social situation. They may have also had parents or siblings who were socially anxious and may have grown up in an overly protective or critical environment. Other people may remember a certain period of time when their problem in social situations started. Sometimes they report a very uncomfortable speaking event that precipitated their problem. In other cases, fear of social situations and failure gradually grew stronger over the years as the social demands to perform became more and more important.

There is no single psychological theory that can conclusively explain why some people develop social anxiety but not others. Your genes, upbringing, and previous experiences all contribute to varying degrees. There is some indication in the literature that SAD is associated with structural and metabolic brain differences. Imagine your brain is like a house. At the bottom is the basement with a furnace, the electric circuit breakers, the plumbing, and so on, and on the top floors are the living quarters, offices, kitchen, et cetera. As is true for a house, the bottom of the brain was built first, by evolution, and represents the more primitive and evolutionarily conserved areas, whereas the top of the brain houses the frontal areas of the cortex. Some research on SAD found evidence of abnormalities in the stress response. This research suggests that there is too much activity of so-called "bottom-up brain regions" involved in processing emotions and too little activity of so-called "top-down" brain regions involved in cognitive appraisal and emotion regulation (Phan and Klumpp 2014). Other research has found abnormalities in the functioning of neurotransmitters, molecules that send information from one neuron to another in the brain. Based on the results of pharmacotherapy studies, it appears that SAD is associated with an imbalance of some these neurotransmitters (Blanco et al. 2014).

We also know that family members seem to show a shared risk for social anxiety, which suggests that there is a genetic contribution to social anxiety. If your parents are socially anxious people, you are more likely to develop social anxiety than somebody whose parents are not socially anxious. The genetic disposition to develop SAD is closely connected to certain temperament variables. In particular, shyness, one of the most heritable temperament factors, is closely related to SAD. The late Jerome Kagan, a developmental psychologist from Harvard, believed that social anxiety is closely related to a temperamental variable that occurs in early childhood called *behavioral inhibition*. Behavioral inhibition is defined as an inhibited or avoidant behavioral response to unfamiliar and unexpected events. It is directly linked to a low threshold of excitability of the amygdala, a small brain structure involved in the emotional processing of information. Studies have found that behavioral inhibition in childhood, an early sign of shyness, is closely associated with social anxiety and SAD in adolescence (Kagan 2014a, b). Children with this trait display fearfulness, timidity, and wariness when encountering novel people, objects, or events. Kagan and his colleagues also found that parents of children who were inhibited at twenty-one months of age were significantly more likely to meet diagnostic criteria for SAD (17.5%) than parents of uninhibited children (0%) and parents whose children were neither inhibited nor uninhibited (2.9%).

However, a large number of people who were shy or behaviorally inhibited as children do not develop SAD later on during adulthood. This suggests that SAD is caused by a number of factors, and that people may also be protected from becoming socially anxious by numerous other factors, including family and peer relationships, other personality traits, and cultural factors (Henderson et al. 2014). The highest rates of SAD are reported in the Americas, New Zealand, and Australia, whereas the lowest are reported in Asian countries (Brockveld et al. 2014). The reason for these cultural differences might be that Western cultures tend to place a greater value on extraverted and individualistic behaviors, whereas East Asian cultures value more quiet and introverted styles (Hofmann et al. 2010).

In sum, the literature suggests that social anxiety—along with its precursors, shyness and behavioral inhibition—runs in families and is more prevalent in certain cultures. There are many possible reasons why you might be struggling with this problem. Social anxiety is at least partly due to genetic factors. However, this does not mean that you can't effectively target it with psychological interventions. Quite the opposite. There are very effective and fairly straightforward strategies that will allow you to take back your life. Sarah, Joseph, and Carrie are different people with a different history, different weaknesses, different strengths, and different resources. Yet all share a similar problem—social anxiety—expressed in different ways and caused by different factors. But the reasons why your social anxiety developed in the first place (the initiating factors) are often very different from the reasons why a problem still exists (the maintaining factors). We will say more about this in the next chapter. It turns out that those maintaining factors respond very well to psychological treatments, even if the initiating factors may be biological or even genetic in nature. This book will teach you strategies to target the various maintaining factors for your social anxiety with the goal to get your life back. Some of these strategies will be more relevant than others for your individual problem. In order to determine which strategy is most effective, I encourage you to try them all out first and then to go back to the ones that seem to be most effective. Be patient and kind to yourself. But also be persistent. You will see that they will work!

CHAPTER 2

And It Keeps On Going and Going...But Why?

When something isn't right, we naturally try to understand the cause, because sometimes, knowing the cause tells us how to fix it. But very often the reasons why a problem started and the reasons why a problem persists are two very different things. In fact, more important than knowing the reasons why your social anxiety started in the first place (the initiating factors) is to know the reasons why it is still there (the maintaining factors). Factors that initially cause a problem are rarely, if ever, the same as those that maintain a problem. And conversely, knowing the factors that maintain a problem tells you almost nothing about the factors that initially caused the problem.

For example, if you go to your doctor with a broken arm, they will take X-rays and put it in a cast. It is irrelevant whether you broke your arm because you fell down from your apple tree, because of a ski accident, or because a friend talked you into bungee jumping. The treatment is the same, no matter what the initial reason for the problem is. In other words, in order to effectively treat a problem (pain in arm), it is important to know what maintains the problem (broken bone), and not what created it in the first place (type of accident). This is not to say that the problem history is unimportant or irrelevant. Rather, it is not essential in order to find ways to correct it.

To make matters even more complicated, an effective treatment tells you little about the initiating factors, and more than one treatment can eliminate a problem via different mechanisms. For example, if you have a really bad headache, you may take some aspirin. This does not mean that there are some "aspirin sensors" in your brain that detect that you have some sort of "aspirin deficiency." Rather, aspirin inhibits the actions of particular hormone-like substances (prostaglandins) involved in injury and inflammation that intensify the pain signal. You could probably also have gotten rid of your headache through other drugs, or maybe even just by taking a nap, doing some relaxation exercises, eating, or drinking caffeine.

Therefore, factors that initially create the problem (such as personality characteristics, past experiences, learning environment) are not the same as the factors that still maintain the problem. Treatments for social anxieties work because they target the maintaining factors. Typically, there are a number of factors responsible for why the problem is still maintained. Therefore, different treatments work because they eliminate different maintaining factors. In this chapter, we will discuss some of the most important factors that lead to the maintenance of social anxiety. First, though, let me give you a very succinct summary. It's okay if not everything makes sense right away. It will become clear as we home in on these different aspect.

Maintaining Factors

Social anxiety, the fear of social situations, is something really interesting. You are constantly confronted with social situations in your daily life. Just think about how often you interact with people during your day. And yet, in the absence of treatment, social anxiety can persist for many years or decades. What keeps this anxiety going? Why don't people get used to it? Over the last two decades, my colleagues and I have drilled into this issue. We did a lot of research, integrated the existing literature and studies, and derived a comprehensive maintenance model of SAD (Hofmann 2007; Hofmann and Otto 2008).

At the heart of SAD is a big feedback loop that starts at social apprehensions and loops back with avoidance. It starts with being in an anxiety-provoking social situation. You feel apprehensive in this situation in part because you perceive a high standard for social acceptance. You want to make a good impression on others while you doubt you will be able to do so, partly because you are unable to define goals and select specific achievable behavioral strategies to reach these goals. This leads to a further increase of your social apprehension and also to increased self-focused attention, which then triggers a number of closely interrelated cognitive responses. Specifically, you exaggerate the likelihood of social mishaps and the potential social costs involved in social situations. You might assume that you are in danger of behaving in an inept and unacceptable fashion and believe that this will result in disastrous consequences, such as being ostracized from a valued group. You might feel as though you have very little control over your anxiety response in social situations and exaggerate the visibility of your anxiety response to other people, which will most likely increase your fear of behaving in an unacceptable manner and fuel fears of rejection.

As you can see, these responses are closely associated with each other and with a tendency to perceive oneself negatively in social situations. The activation of one factor leads to another, all of which add up to more social anxiety. As a result, you might engage in avoidance and/or safety behaviors, followed by post-event rumination, such as going to a party but only talking to your close friends, or replaying every conversation that you had the next day. This cycle feeds on itself, ultimately leading to the maintenance and further exacerbation of the problem.

Figure 2 shows these various possible maintaining factors and how they influence each other. Some factors are more important for some people than for others. But you might be able to relate to many, if not all, of these maintaining factors.

For example, let's assume that Sarah is about to give a speech. As she is standing in front of the audience, she can feel her anxiety building up. She wants to give a perfect presentation and impress people, but she knows that she can't do it. She doesn't even know how she could do it (i.e., her perceived social standard is high, while her social goal is poorly defined). She feels social apprehension and anxiety leading her to focus her attention toward her own body and her own self (i.e., she experiences heightened self-focused attention directed toward negative aspects of herself). She believes that it will be a catastrophe if she messes things up (i.e., she shows high estimated social cost), thinks that she has little control over her anxiety (i.e., she perceives her emotional control as being low), and thinks that she

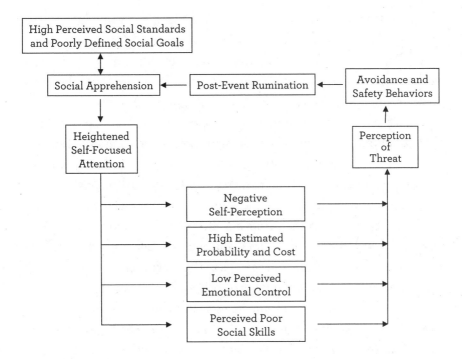

Figure 2: Maintenance of SAD. From Hofmann, Stefan G. 2007. "Cognitive Factors That Maintain Social Anxiety Disorder: A Comprehensive Model and Its Treatment Implications." *Cognitive Behaviour Therapy* 36: 195–209. doi: 10.1080/16506070701421313. Reprinted with permission.

a bad public speaker (i.e., she perceives her social skills as being poor). This, in turn, increases her perception of threat, which causes her to speak quickly to get out of the situation as soon as possible (i.e., she avoids her fear). After the speech, she continues to ruminate over it, further increasing her social apprehension of those types of situations.

Let's walk through this cycle in more detail, step by step. First, a social situation is in part anxiety provoking because the goals that you want to achieve in the situation are high, or because you assume that the social standard is high. If nobody expected anything from you or if everybody performed very poorly, you would feel considerably less social apprehension than if everybody expected a lot from you, and your goals were very high. If this is an important maintaining factor for you (meaning that your goals and your assumption of social standards are high), you will need to target this by realizing that in general people do not expect as much from you as you think they do. Furthermore, you will have to learn how to define clear goals for yourself during a social situation and how to use this information to determine whether or not you were successful.

Once you experience initial social apprehension, attention is typically directed inwardly—toward self-evaluation and toward sensations of anxiety. We know that this shift in attention makes the problem worse. If this is what's happening to you, you are spending your precious mental resources scanning your body and examining yourself as well as trying to handle the situation. In order to intervene effectively, you will need to learn strategies to direct your attention away from your anxious feelings and toward the situation in order to successfully complete the social task.

You may focus your attention inwardly and notice aspects about yourself that you don't like when being in a social situation. In other words, you may perceive yourself negatively and believe that everybody else shares the same distorted and negative beliefs with you. "I am such an inhibited idiot" is an example of a self-statement that reflects negative self-perception, and you can see how this thought might lead you to believe that others feel the same way. It is important that you become comfortable with the way you are (including your imperfections in social performance situations). You will need to learn strategies to change this negative view of yourself and become comfortable with the way you are. You will also need to realize that other people do not share the same negative view as you.

Major social mishaps with serious consequences are rare. Minor social mishaps are normal and happen all the time. Some social mishaps are even endearing, making the person more likable. But what makes people different is the degree to which these mishaps affect a person's life. You may believe that social mishaps have disastrous consequences for you. For example, you might think that giving a bad speech would cause you to get fired and that nobody would want to hire you again, ending your career for good. In order to deal with social anxiety effectively, you will need to realize that even if a social encounter objectively did not go well, it is no big deal. Catastrophes can happen, but they are very rare. Getting killed is a catastrophe. But getting rejected by a date or giving a bad speech is not a catastrophe.

You may notice the bodily symptoms of your anxiety a lot when you are in a socially threatening situation. You may feel panic-like anxiety that appears to get out of your control, and you may think that everybody around you can see and sense your racing heart, dry mouth, sweaty palms, and so on. To deal with your social anxiety effectively, you will need to realize that you have more control over your anxious feelings than you think. Reexamining your perception can help you calm your bodily response. You will also need to realize that you overestimate how much other people can see what's going on in your body. Your feeling of anxiety is a very private experience; other people cannot see your racing heart, your sweaty palms, or your shaky knees.

You may further believe that your social skills are inadequate to deal with a social situation. For example, you might believe that you're a naturally bad speaker and, therefore, feel very uncomfortable in most public speaking situations. As an intervention, I would want to make you realize that your actual social performance is not nearly as bad as you think it is, and that poor skills are not the reason for your discomfort in social situations. In fact, there are plenty of people in this world whose social skills are much more limited that yours but who are not socially anxious.

As a result of all these processes, you use avoidance strategies. You may avoid the situation, escape, or use strategies that make you less uncomfortable. All of these activities (or lack thereof) are intended to avoid the feeling of anxiety. As an intervention, you will want to learn that using avoidance strategies (either active or passive) is part of the reason why your social anxiety is so persistent, because you never know what would happen if you did not avoid the situation.

But the problem doesn't stop here, even after the situation has passed. You may tend to ruminate a lot about a social situation after it is over. You might focus not only on the negative aspects, but also on ambiguous parts (things that could be interpreted as negative or positive), which you may tend to interpret negatively. Again, this only makes the situation much worse. To intervene effectively, you will need to realize that ruminating about past situations is a bad idea. What happened, happened; time to move on. Ruminating only makes things worse and makes you more anxious and avoidant about future situations. Some of this information is rather complex. But so is your anxiety. Let's discuss these maintaining factors in more detail next.

Social Standards

Anxiety arises in social situations when a person wishes to convey a desired impression but is unsure about their ability to do so. This wish is often linked to the natural desire to belong to a desired group and to adhere to the social norms of a particular culture, which, by the way, stands in direct opposition to psychopathic individuals who do not care about social norms. In other words, while psychopaths don't care about others, people with SAD care too much. If the world consisted only of people with SAD, it would be a much kinder world, but it would also be a very anxious and lonely world full of avoidance.

We know that people with SAD often show a discrepancy between perceived social standards and their perceived social abilities. This discrepancy was found to be largely due to the individuals' underestimation of their ability level in relation to the perceived social standard and desired goals. The following dissertation study by one of my former students brings home this point by looking at how the self-perception of people with SAD as "deficient" gets activated by contexts in which others' standards are seen as being either high or unclear (Moscovitch and Hofmann 2006). In other words, if you have social anxiety, it is likely triggered by situations in which the standards are either high (like with a friend who values competition) or unclear (like with a boss who gives intermittent feedback).

In this study, thirty-nine individuals with SAD and thirty-nine non-clinical controls (i.e., individuals without a diagnosis of SAD) performed a public speech after receiving cues about social standards. One third of participants received cues indicating that standards for performance were high, one third received cues that standards were low, and the remaining third were given no explicit information about expected standards (i.e., standards were ambiguous). Allow me to give you some details about this study so you can appreciate how scientists study phenomena like these in an experiment.

Participants in this study were told that they would be required to give an impromptu ten-minute videotaped speech on randomly chosen topics. They were informed that the speech would be observed by the experimenter and that the video would later be evaluated by other people. After hearing these initial instructions, participants rated their predicted level of performance and perceived audience standards, each on a 0–10 scale. They were then randomly assigned to one of three experimental conditions: *high standards*, *low standards*, and *no standards*. In each condition, participants viewed a video clip of an individual speaking for two minutes about "tourist attractions in Boston." The individual featured in the video clip was a volunteer in our laboratory whose speech was planned and recorded prior to the experiment, although participants were not privy to this information until the conclusion of the study. Participants received a scripted set of oral instructions over the intercom prior to watching the video clip.

All participants actually viewed *the same* video clip; however, the oral instructions they received with the video differed across the three experimental conditions. The script for the *high standards* condition contained the following information: "In our experience, people prefer to watch another person perform a task before they have to do it themselves. So, before you give your speech, I would like you to get a sense of what the task will be like by showing you an example of a speech on video. As you watch the short video clip, keep in mind that not all speech performances are alike. A lot of different people have participated in this experiment before you, from both our Center and the community at large, and they have shown a wide range of anxiety and performance abilities. Truthfully, most people have performed quite a bit better than the individual in the video that you will now watch. Nevertheless, this video clip should still give you a good sense of what the task will be like."

In the *low standards* condition, participants received instructions that were identical to those given to the *high standards* participants, except they were told that "most people have not performed quite as well as the individual in the video that you will now watch." In the *no standards* condition, participants viewed the video without receiving any information about performance demands or expectations. Participants were told that they were watching the video in order to assess their level of concentration, and instructions directed their attention to superficial aspects of the video. In the *no standards* script, participants were asked to count the times the person used the word "Boston."

Participants were then asked to speak for a maximum of ten minutes but were allowed to terminate their speech at any time by raising a "stop" sign in the air. Participants were told that the speech topics were chosen randomly (however, the topics for all participants were *capital punishment*, *abortion*, and *cloning*), and they were asked to hold the paper containing the topics face down (i.e., not to look at the topics) until they began their speech. Following their speech, participants rated their own performance on a 0–10 scale and their level of anxiety during the speech on a 0–100 scale. They were then debriefed, compensated for their participation, and dismissed. Two independent raters, blind to the purpose of the study and the condition and diagnostic status of participants, watched and rated the videotaped speeches.

Individuals with SAD thought that their social performance was worse than people without SAD did only when the social standards were high (i.e., when they were made to believe that most other people performed really well) and when the social standards were ambiguous (i.e., when it wasn't made apparent how well most other people performed). Therefore, information about social standards moderates self-appraisals in people with SAD. In the absence of explicit information about expected performance standards (i.e., when standards were ambiguous), people with SAD rated their performance as having been poor—as poor as when performance standards were unambiguously high. On the other hand, when participants were led to believe that expected standards were low, their self-appraisals were indistinguishable from those of controls. Thus, people's perception of themselves as "deficient" seems to become activated by contexts in which others' standards are seen as being either high or unclear.

Unfortunately, daily life is filled with such ambiguous standards, as expressed in the title of our article "Ambiguity Hurts." Accordingly, one target for intervention might involve clarification of actual standards for performance. Dire interpretations of the consequences of imperfect social performances need to be challenged by specifically designed exposures, which we will discuss in chapter 3. During an exposure, you confront yourself with a socially threatening situation in order to test your beliefs. Exposures that test your beliefs about the consequences of a social mishap are termed *social mishap exposures*. These exercises will provide you with direct evidence that (1) the likelihood of social mishaps is small, and, (even more importantly) (2) the consequences of social mishaps (social costs) are neither catastrophic nor unmanageable. But more about this later.

Goal Definition

Social anxiety occurs when you doubt your ability to make a desired impression on other people, or when you feel that you are not able to attain your goals in a social situation. Your personal goals for a social interaction not only determine the demands of a situation, but also influence your thoughts, feelings, and behaviors in a specific way. For example, when going on a job interview, the concrete goal might be to convince interviewers that you are the best fit for the job. However, if you have SAD and regularly think, *I always say something stupid in job interviews*, you might focus more on not saying the wrong thing than fully concentrate on the task and on giving satisfying answers to the interviewer's questions. Anxious thoughts, such as *People will see my anxiety* and *If I blow this one, my life is over* are not helpful and will make it seem like you are distracted, unqualified, or disinterested in a job you could, in fact, perform admirably and really want.

Interventions designed to help people with SAD set objective and attainable goals for social situations and are designed to address both elevated social standards and diffuse, unrealistic, or subjective goals. This involves examining whether your goals are objective and do not involve "mind reading" others' judgments of your social adequacy. In this way, improving your goal setting will provide the dual benefits of (1) helping you "get out of the heads" of others and define what is truly needed from a social interaction or performance, while (2) defining an adequate level of performance relative to a specified situation. In the case of a job interview, this means that the goal is not to appear brilliant, ingenious, or irresistible. This would be an example of an unattainable goal. Rather, the goal might be to inform your interviewer about your relevant job experience and the skills that make you qualified for the job. Concerns about your interviewer's assessment of your personal character is not overly relevant for this task— and focusing on this will interfere with your success in obtaining the job.

Self-Focused Attention

When confronted with a social threat, socially anxious individuals shift their attention inwardly and engage in a process of detailed monitoring and observation of themselves. When their self-focused attention is high, they experience spontaneous, recurrent, and excessively negative self-images, which they believe to be accurate at the time they occur. The negative self-image is not limited to how they perceive themselves socially, but it can also include physical attributes, including bodily appearance. Improving social anxiety, therefore, often also leads to a reduction of these concerns.

These negative self-images are causally related to social anxiety. Compared to non-anxious people, individuals with SAD are more likely to "see" themselves in social situations as if from an observer's perspective. When instructed to focus their attention on aspects of the external environment, individuals with SAD report less anxiety and fewer negative beliefs. Moreover, SAD makes people exaggerate the negative aspects of a situation and dismiss the positive aspects and, if things can be interpreted either way, to interpret them as negative. Catching a smile from a person could mean that somebody is thinking you're ridiculous or that the person likes you. A quiet audience could mean that you are able to capture their attention or that you are boring them. And if you see one person in the audience nodding off, you could think, *I am boring people to death* or *He is not interested in my talk* or *This person had a late night and is tired*. Depending on your interpretation, you will experience different emotions, and some of these emotions can further increase your anxiety. For example, the thought "I am boring people to death" will lead to even greater anxiety. In contrast, the thought "This person had a late night and is tired" won't capture much of your attention and will have little influence on your anxiety.

In treatment, I often teach my patients to voluntarily focus their attention on different things in order to train attentional control. For example, right before a social performance task (such as a public speech), I might instruct them to focus their attention inwardly on their anxiety, or outwardly, such as on specific objects in the room, or on their speech topic. As they do this, I might ask them to notice their anxiety, which is typically the greatest when focusing on the anxiety and less when focusing on a neutral object in the room, such as chair. The objective of this exercise is not only to demonstrate a link between attentional focus and anxiety, but also to show that attention allocation is under our own voluntary control. If we have the power to make things worse (when focusing on our anxiety), we also have the power to make things easier. Changes in anxiety from this exercise shows that anxiety is not an automatic and fixed response to social situations, but rather is a function of subjective and modifiable attentional factors.

Self-Perception

Self-perception is a very common maintaining factor of SAD. You experience social anxiety if you think that you are unable to convey a desired impression of yourself to important other people. It is possible that early learning experiences were responsible for developing a number of distorted, negative assumptions about yourself (e.g., "I'm stupid," "I'm unattractive"). In a series of well-controlled studies, Lynn Alden and her colleagues at the University of British Columbia in Vancouver, Canada, examined the effect of self-perception on anxiety in individuals with SAD (Alden et al. 2014). These studies showed that when faced with social threat, socially anxious individuals shift their attention inward and engage in a process of detailed self-monitoring during which they experience spontaneous, recurrent, and excessively negative self-images that they perceive as being accurate. When exposed to social threat, people with SAD tend to underestimate their abilities relative to others' standards. They are concerned that others may hold high standards for their performance in social situations, and this concern may significantly influence their emotions and behavior.

Alden and her colleagues also observed that people with SAD who receive feedback that they performed well during a social encounter react with *increased* anxiety when anticipating a subsequent encounter due to their perception that their initial success may have led evaluators to raise expected performance standards. Similarly, when individuals with social anxiety perceive expected standards to be unreachable, they may employ the strategy of purposeful failure in order to influence potential evaluators to lower their performance expectations to a level they can more confidently match. In other words, self-sabotage is not an atypical response to successful social performance for some people with SAD. Appearing incompetent is a sure way keep you out of the spotlight.

In addition, individuals with SAD form negative mental self-representations based not on how they view themselves but on how they believe potential "audience" evaluators view them at any given moment. In other words, people with SAD feel that they are constantly on stage and seem to hold biased, negative self-appraisals. This might even occur outside a social context and regardless of their level of skill or the degree of warmth and friendliness exhibited by their interaction partners. This might be the reason for the relatively high overlap between SAD and depression. As an intervention, video feedback can serve as a particularly effective tool to correct negative and distorted self-perception. Viewing your own video-taped performance can initiate a change in your self-perception when you are given the opportunity to evaluate your own objective social performance and contrast it to the way you subjectively experienced your performance in the moment. Video recordings using your smartphone offer an easy way to view your own performance. Other alternatives are mirror exposures (i.e., looking at yourself repeatedly in the mirror without engaging in checking behaviors, such as "I wonder if my nose is too big") and repeated exposure to your own recorded voice. I will present the specific techniques at a later time. For now, just know that your social anxiety likely leads you to be much harder on yourself than other people are on you, and that this book will help you learn how to be kinder to yourself.

Estimated Social Cost

Flying a Boeing 747 with 416 passengers on board requires some skills and can be a scary task. Making a mistake during the landing operation can result in some serious negative consequences. For example, the plane could crash and the 416 passengers on board plus crew members could die. That would be a catastrophe with serious long-term negative and irreversible consequences. Unless you believe in the afterlife, once you're dead, you're dead. Compare this to a social task, such as a public speaking event. Similar to the landing procedure of a flight, a public speech also requires some skills. However, making a mistake during a speech or any other social task does not result in similarly negative long-term and irreversible consequences. Public speakers or their audience members do not die, regardless of how bad a speech it is. Unpleasant situations happen all the time. They are uncomfortable, they are distressing, but people forget and forgive and move on with their lives. Social situations, no matter how bad they end up, are not catastrophes. Yet, people with SAD do not see it that way, as shown by research studies.

British psychologists David Clark and Adrian Wells formulated an influential cognitive theory of SAD (Clark and Wells 1995) stating that individuals with SAD believe that (1) they may behave in an inept and unacceptable fashion, and (2) that such behavior would have disastrous consequences in terms of loss of status, loss of worth, and rejection. The second part of this theory has since been termed "estimated social cost" and is closely tied to an influential and earlier model of fear and anxiety by Edna Foa at the University of Pennsylvania and the late Michael Kozak (Foa and Kozak 1986). This model assumes that a person's response to treatment for various anxiety problems partly depends on their ability to reduce the exaggerated probabilities and cost associated with the feared consequences of a situation. Let me explain.

Fear and anxiety problems are represented in something called a *fear structure* (a cognitive network where fear is represented in the form or thoughts, behaviors, and physiology). If a person's fear structure is completely activated (e.g., by being exposed to the feared object or situation) and they experience no negative consequences, they can learn to reduce their tendency to exaggerate probability estimates of harm. Habituation of anxiety during exposure (i.e., the learning that occurs as a result of repeated presentations of a threat) would then reduce inflated estimated social cost if the person attributes the decline of their anxiety to characteristics of the social situation (e.g., *If I am not anxious, the situation cannot be so bad*).

The outcome of a social situation is not always clear or predictable. Often, there is no consequence at all; sometimes, the consequence is unexpectedly positive; and other times it's negative. Unexpected positive consequences are often dismissed or reinterpreted negatively (as we will discuss in more detail later when we examine post-event rumination). Negative consequences are manifold. An example of a negative consequence might be getting some criticism from the audience about your speech. This will impact you differently, depending on the context. For example, if repeated exposure to criticism no longer evokes physiological arousal, then you will no longer perceive being criticized as disastrous. According to Foa and Kozak, compared to non-anxious people, those with SAD are similarly accurate at estimating the likelihood that social mishaps might happen, but they tend to overestimate the potentially negative consequences of those mishaps, often assuming that they have long-lasting, negative, and irreversible effects on their lives. This could mean that psychological treatments for SAD are effective in part *because* they lead to the lowering of one's social cost estimate. If this is the case, we have identified one of the mechanisms through which cognitive behavioral therapy (CBT) works. The variables that make up a therapy mechanism are often called *treatment mediators*.

The first direct evidence for the role of estimated social cost as a treatment mediator for SAD comes from one of Foa's studies (Foa et al. 1996). Before and after receiving CBT, the authors asked people with SAD to rate the likelihood that a bad event would happen (to measure estimated probabilities of bad events) and also asked them to estimate how bad the consequences would be (to measure their social cost estimates). In addition, they gathered the same kind of data from a group of non-anxious people. The results were consistent with Foa and Kozak's hypothesis that individuals with SAD exhibit specific judgmental biases for the costs of negative social events. Participants also evidenced socially relevant judgmental biases prior to treatment, which were attenuated following treatment. Specifically, they showed a decrease in both estimated costs and overestimation of the probability of negative social events, which correlated with a decrease in the severity of their symptoms after treatment. This suggests that estimated costs were the best single predictor for treatment outcome based on Foa and Kozak's mediation model. This effect was later replicated in other studies, including my own (Hofmann 2004), which also showed that direct cognitive intervention leads to better maintenance of treatment gains, and this effect was mediated via changes in estimated social cost during treatment.

Although certain cognitive strategies in more traditional CBT approaches address this issue to some degree, the treatment effect can often be improved when aggressively targeting estimated social cost in specific ways. For example, when you repeatedly and continuously expose yourself to a socially threatening situation, your anxiety decreases not only because of habituation, but also because you realize that the feared outcome is not going to happen and if it happens, that you can handle it. This effect can be enhanced if you identify and challenge your exaggerated cost estimation (e.g., *What would be the worst outcome of this situation? Why is this situation such a catastrophic event? How will my life change as a result of this event?*). What's more, social mishaps are quite normal, and the negative consequences of such mishaps are usually short lasting. During the planning stage of an exposure practice, which we'll discuss in chapter 3, I'll encourage you to create social mishaps in order to examine the actual consequences. These exposures can help you realize, first, that perfect performance need never be the standard for social acceptability or safety, and second, through repeated and vivid experiences of committing social mishaps, that these mishaps need not and should not be interpreted catastrophically.

After many decades of research and treating people with SAD, I have come to realize that mishap exposures (sometimes also referred to as social cost exposures) are often essential for many people with SAD to overcome their social anxiety (Fang et al. 2013, for further elaboration). It has also become clear that these interventions have specific value for relapse prevention, not only by establishing new patterns of social attention, goal setting, and performance evaluations, but also by setting a standard for the notable distinction between social failure and social mishaps; the latter can occur with no important social consequences.

Perception of Emotional Control

Your host just introduced you. You're standing in front of a microphone. The lights are shining on you. The audience is getting quiet, expecting you to start your speech. Your heart is racing. You can hear you heart pounding. Your palms are sweating. Your anxiety is out of control. As with many emotional disorders, social anxiety disorder is frequently associated with a perception of a lack of control over aversive events (such as a public speech or a party), which can result in subjective, behavioral, and physiological distress. The degree to which we view events as within our control is a fundamental aspect—and even determinant—of our mental health. My friend and former mentor, David Barlow, has contributed greatly to this insight (Barlow 2001). He observed that unexpected and uncontrollable bursts of fear can lead to anxiety disorders in vulnerable individuals because they view their own emotions or bodily reactions as out of control. This is quite evident in people with panic disorder. This disorder can develop when individuals unexpectedly experience brief and intense bursts of fear and subsequently develop anxiety over the possibility of this response reoccurring in an uncontrollable manner. But this is not at all unique to panic disorder. In fact, Barlow discovered that all anxiety disorders, including social anxiety disorder, share a lack of perceived control over negative emotional and bodily reactions. For example, one of my early studies (Hofmann et al. 1995) showed that people who are afraid of public speaking attributed their fear more often to "panic attacks" (defined as a sudden rush of intense fear without apparent reason) than to traumatic events or any other events. Although all participants in this study met diagnostic criteria for SAD, they regarded panic attacks as more important for their speech anxiety than their fear of negative evaluation by others (which is considered the core feature of SAD). A more recent study (Hofmann 2005) with a large and representative sample of people with SAD showed that situations with high estimated social cost produce anxiety in part because people perceive their anxiety symptoms as being out of control.

These and other studies show that the perception of control over one's anxiety response associated with threatening events is highly related to treatment gains in SAD. This is also known as emotion-focused coping (i.e., referring to the strategies we apply to regulate our emotions). The more we believe we are in control over our emotions and our anxiety, the better we can handle threatening situations. Therefore, social exposures should be designed to put your core social fears to the test. For example, you may combine exposure to anxiety-producing social cues with exposure to feared anxiety sensations designed to redefine the "danger" and "safety" of these anxiety sensations.

Perceived Social Skills

The world is never under our complete personal control, and most activities carry some potential risks. Some activities are riskier than others. Wingsuit BASE jumping (the crazy sport where people jump off cliffs to start gliding in their wingsuit) is riskier than taking an easy stroll around your neighborhood. But even the stroll carries some risks. You might get hit by a car, for example. Sure, it's not very likely, but it's not impossible. It could happen. The inherent danger of a situation also depends on your skills to deal with a threat. The very first time you jumped off the cliff in your BASE jumping class was riskier than your fiftieth time because your skills to handle threat gradually built with experience. But there is a difference between your *actual* skills and your *perceived* skills. Your actual skills are obvious to others. Your perceived skills are the skills you believe you have.

The sense of competence in mastering something has a name: perceived self-efficacy. This concept was studied in great detail by Albert Bandura (who sadly passed away days before I wrote these words), one of the most highly cited psychological scientists ever. Bandura started studying the role of perceived self-efficacy on anxiety reduction during treatment (Bandura 1988). After much research and many revisions of the concept, perceived self-efficacy is now defined as the belief that we can exercise control over potential threats. To take it one step further, the higher your perceived self-efficacy, the higher your sense of predictability and controllability of anxiety-provoking events. It turns out that perceived self-efficacy plays a central role in anxiety. A threat of a situation is related to the person's belief about how well they can manage it. Remember the first time you sat in a car when you began learning to drive? Controlling the car's speed with your gas pedal while watching the traffic and steering was certainly anxiety producing. Your driving skills had to be learned and practiced. Your anxiety was high because your perceived self-efficacy was low. With practice, your anxiety decreased as your perceived self-efficacy increased. Therefore, the belief that we have some control determines our level of anxiety. Translated to SAD, the way to cope with social threat is by dealing with our anxiety arousal (i.e., the emotion-focused coping that we discussed in the previous section) and by our belief regarding how much we are able to manage the demands of the social situation with our social skills (i.e., problem-focused coping). It is important here to stress that it is the *perception* of skills that matters.

People with SAD are not clearly deficient in any of their social skills. However, they often tend to appraise their own performance in social situations more negatively. If, as a result of using the strategies in this book, you perceive your social skills as improved, or as better than you originally thought, social situations would then appear less threatening and dangerous because you would have an increased sense of control over the situation. Subsequently, you might end up performing better in terms of your social goals because of the diminished social anxiety. In other words, reducing social anxiety makes you more confident and less fearful of future social situations, enhancing your perceived social skills to manage potential social threats.

I have studied many hundreds of people with SAD, often in the context of treatment studies. Most people were clearly not deficient in their social skills. Only very few had clear deficits in their social skills. Some of them were unable to maintain eye contact, showed awkward behaviors, spoke too softly or too fast, stuttered, were inappropriate by trying to be funny, or were even aggressive. For those individuals, social skills training is suitable. But for the majority of people with SAD, social skills training is rather inappropriate because it reinforces their perfectionistic tendency and their perception of being incapable of reaching their social goals and meeting the perceived social standard. The perception of one's social skills is an aspect of a person's self-perception and can be addressed using techniques such as video feedback, audio feedback, mirror exposure, and group feedback.

Safety and Avoidance Behaviors

Safety behaviors are a form of avoidance. Earlier I defined avoidance as anything you do or do not do to avoid feeling your anxiety. This may include choosing not to go to the dreaded party or leaving the meeting early. In both cases, these behaviors reduce your anxiety by eliminating the threat. But some behaviors are much more subtle. For example, you may avoid eye contact with people at the party, stay close to the exit door during a gathering, or overprepare your speech. All of these behaviors are also intended to reduce your anxiety. These are more subtle than not going into a situation or escaping a situation. Therefore, we call these behaviors *safety behaviors*. The name implies that they make you feel safe, thereby reducing your level of distress.

Although these behaviors reduce your anxiety in the short term, they also maintain your anxiety in the long term. We will discuss this in greater detail in the following chapters. We do know that avoidance behaviors are important contributors to your maintenance of social anxiety and that using safety behaviors undermines the effects of adaptive ways to cope with social threat. This is because avoidance and safety behaviors prevent you from evaluating the real threat of a social situation. As long as you avoid, you forfeit the chance to experience that the situation is not as dangerous as you believe it to be and that you do have some control over it. Do you still remember learning to ride a bicycle? As long as you rode the bicycle with training wheels, you never gave yourself a chance to know that you could ride it without them. Eventually, you had to take your training wheels off in order to know that it's safe to ride without them. In the same way a person with SAD might think, *Who knows what would have happened if I did not have my [safety behavior] to rely on?*

Safety behaviors are subtle forms of avoidance strategies and are notoriously difficult to catch. Using particular phrases or filler words during your speech, always having a drink in your hand at a party even if you are not drinking anything, or holding your drink very tightly to avoid trembling, and standing close to the exit at a group gathering in order to get out more easily are all examples. They all serve the function of making you less uncomfortable in a socially threatening situation. You might not even be aware that the things you do are safety behaviors. In order to identify them, you will first need to monitor your social encounters and become a detective of your own problems. You need to remain vigilant for signs of any such safety behaviors. Once you identify them, the next step is to systematically eliminate them. For this, you will need to generate exposure tasks as an opportunity to learn that that social situations are actually quite safe.

Planning for exposures involves creating the situations where your beliefs about the "dangerousness" of social situations are directly challenged. These exposures typically involve experiencing social mishaps, inducing anxiety-like symptoms, and practicing—in multiple contexts— eliminating safety cues and behaviors. This helps you redefine social situations as "safe," even if you don't use those safety cues and behaviors.

Post-Event Rumination

Imagine the following scenario. You are at a party and somebody introduces you to Kim. You really like Kim and, in a rare moment of great courage, you ask her for her phone number to meet up for coffee sometime. To your surprise, Kim says, "Sure, why don't you give me a call sometime." After you get back to your safe home, you still can't believe what just happened. You asked this person for her phone number and she actually gave it to you! You experience a mix of pleasant and unpleasant emotions—joy, exhilaration, and fright. Now what? Will you call her? You replay the scene in your mind over and over again. Kim's voice and words are still in your head. She said, "Sure, why don't you give me a call sometime." As you rehearse the scene over and over, your emotions turn from bright to dark. She said "sure." She didn't say "great" or "wonderful." "Sure" is not as positive as "great" or wonderful." "Sure" is just okay. And then she said, "Why don't you give me a call sometime." What did Kim mean by "sometime"? Sometime could also mean never. Oh, what a disaster!

You become convinced that Kim does not want you to call her. She probably just wanted to be nice. And slowly but surely, this surprisingly happy situation is turning into a catastrophe in your mind. This is what we call "post-event rumination." The event was getting the phone number, and your ruminating acts turned this positive scene into a negative one.

People with SAD frequently engage in such post-event processing, during which they mentally review the social interaction in detail. This processing typically centers on anxious feelings and negative self-perceptions, in which the individual recalls the interaction as being more negative than it actually was. As a result, their thoughts are dominated by the recollections of past failures, leading to the maintenance of the problem. Such post-event rumination is often associated with avoidance of similar social situations in the future. Post-event rumination may be closely associated with exaggerated social cost in SAD. This occurs when individuals with SAD ruminate about a past social encounter because they believe that an inadequate social performance leads to disastrous consequences. Post-event rumination frequently occurs after an unsuccessful or ambiguously successful social encounter, especially those that are associated with high-perceived social costs and negative self-perception, because of the assumed catastrophic outcome of a social situation.

What Maintaining Factors Are Most Relevant for You?

Chances are you can relate to many, if not all, of these maintaining factors. However, people differ in what maintains their social anxiety. The rating scale below summarizes all known maintaining factors (one item per factor). This scale is intended to give you a guide for focusing more on some strategies in this book than on others depending on the maintaining factor most relevant for you.

Approach to Social Situations Scale

From Hofmann, Stefan G. 2007. "Cognitive Factors That Maintain Social Anxiety Disorder: A Comprehensive Model and Its Treatment Implications." *Cognitive Behaviour Therapy* 36: 195–209. doi: 10.1080/16506070701421313. Reprinted with permission.

Please get a piece of paper and a pen (or use your smartphone) and rate the following statements as honestly as you can. Rate how much you agree with each statement on a scale from 0 (I don't agree at all/this is not typical of me) to 10 (I agree very much/this is very typical of me). The relevant maintaining factor is indicated in parentheses for each item.

1. I believe that the expectations of me in social situations are very high. (perceived social standards)

    0—1—2—3—4—5—6—7—8—9—10

2. I am often not quite clear about what I personally want to achieve in a social situation. (goal definition)

    0—1—2—3—4—5—6—7—8—9—10

3. I tend to focus my attention toward myself when I am in a social situation. (self-focused attention)

    0—1—2—3—4—5—6—7—8—9—10

4. I tend to overestimate how bad a social situation can turn out. (estimated social cost)

    0—1—2—3—4—5—6—7—8—9—10

5. I believe that my social skills to handle social situations are poor. (perceived social skills)

    0—1—2—3—4—5—6—7—8—9—10

6. I don't like myself very much when it comes to social situations. (self-perception)

    0—1—2—3—4—5—6—7—8—9—10

7. I have little control over my anxiety in social situations. (emotional control)

    0—1—2—3—4—5—6—7—8—9—10

8. I think that people can tell when I am anxious in social situations. (perceived social skills)

    0—1—2—3—4—5—6—7—8—9—10

9. I usually expect that something bad will happen to me in a social situation. (estimated social cost)

    0—1—2—3—4—5—6—7—8—9—10

10. I tend to dwell on social situations after they happen. (post-event rumination)

    0—1—2—3—4—5—6—7—8—9—10

11. I often avoid social situations. (safety and avoidance behaviors)

    0—1—2—3—4—5—6—7—8—9—10

12. I often do things that make me feel less uncomfortable when I am in social situations. (safety and avoidance behaviors)

    0—1—2—3—4—5—6—7—8—9—10

Your answers to the questions above will help you determine which chapters will best help you address your social anxiety. If you happen to rate all items highly (5 or greater), all chapters are likely to be very beneficial. Specifically designed exposure strategies, covered in chapter 3, will be essential in general, regardless of which items you rated more highly than others.

The chapters that follow describe specifically designed techniques that focus on some maintaining factors. The *thinking tools* strategies covered in chapter 4 will be quite beneficial for targeting the high perception of social standards (item 1), goal definition (item 2), estimation of social cost (items 4 and 9), self-perception (item 6), and post-event rumination (item 10). The *social mishap exposure* technique described in chapter 5 is an essential core element for all maintaining factors, especially on estimation of social cost (items 4 and 9). The *acceptance skills* you'll learn in chapter 6 are beneficial for targeting self-perception (item 6) and self-focused attention (item 3). The *arousal reduction* exercises in chapter 7 are beneficial for targeting emotional control (item 7), and, finally, the *social skills* strategies in chapter 8 are beneficial for targeting perceived or actual social skills deficits (item 8).

It's important to note that there's not a one-to-one relationship between a specific strategy and a particular maintaining factor. Instead, all strategies touch on virtually all aspects of the maintenance cycle and are designed to provide learning through experiential and cognitive exercises and direct information. So I encourage you to learn and try the strategies presented in all chapters, even if you might ultimately focus on some more than others in your tailored approach to overcoming your social anxiety. And keep in mind, the key to success in all cases is exposure, to which we turn next.

CHAPTER 3

Exposure Is Key

Many children are afraid of dogs, some more than others. Natalie is just terrified of them. Whenever she sees a dog, she gets really panicky. She then hides behind Daddy or runs away screaming. Daddy therefore decided to help Natalie overcome her fear of dogs by gradually confronting her with a number of different and friendly dogs. Every so often when Daddy and Natalie would go for a little walk in the nearby park, Daddy would go up to some friendly looking dogs and their owners and have Natalie interact with the dog. At the beginning, Natalie was very scared, but gradually she became more and more comfortable around dogs. Eventually, she lost her fear completely and was even able to take her neighbors' German shepherd out for a walk. Why? Because fear diminishes with repeated exposure. Natalie simply learned that there is nothing to be afraid of. Fear is like a parasite—it can't live on its own; it can only survive if it is being fed and protected by avoidance.

The critical reader might say, "Yeah, right—this might be true for a child's fear of dogs, but not for the feeling I get when I have to present at meetings in our company." Another reader might say, "This explanation can't be true because I am constantly confronted with social situations in my daily life. And yet, my social anxiety does not get better; rather it gets worse over time."

Social anxiety is clearly a serious problem, and in extreme cases it can be debilitating. The comparison to a child's fear of dogs above is not intended to minimize or trivialize your problem. Instead, this example illus-trates how fear reduction works in principle, and this reaction is the same with your social anxiety as with Natalie's fear of dogs. Studies show that repeated and prolonged confrontation of the feared object or situation in the absence of any avoidance behaviors eventually leads to a decrease in anxious responding. This holds true no matter what the feared object or situation is. Remember how anxious you were when you were learning how to drive a car? Driving a car was no picnic and it's not without danger. But after repeatedly sitting behind the wheel, driving became second nature and your anxiety magically went away with time. However, despite repeated exposures, many people do not experience a decrease in their social anxiety over time because something is preventing this from happening. If this sounds familiar, you might engage in subtle avoidance behaviors, such as overpreparing your speech or holding your drink really tight to avoid using your hand when talking to people. Some of these avoidance strategies can be quite subtle.

What is it that is preventing your social anxiety from decreasing over time? What are those maintaining factors? What keeps it alive? Why haven't you gotten used to it yet? The short answer is twofold: (1) because people with SAD are fearful not so much of the social situation per se, but of the self-attributes (the many perceived flaws) that are activated in these situations (Moscovitch 2009), and (2) because avoidance and negative thoughts lead to the maintenance of social anxiety. For example, if you always avoid going to your friend's annual party, your anxiety about going to this party will remain, simply because avoidance is the main reason for anxiety to be maintained. The long version of this answer is outlined next.

The Good, the Bad, and the Ugly

Anxiety is a normal response. It is adaptive because it protects us from danger. From an evolutionary perspective, having social support is also highly adaptive. Humans are most successful in groups. If our tribe or family had kicked us out, our chance of survival would have been greatly reduced. We would have been easy prey for wild animals and nobody would have been there to help us build our shelter and look for food. Being negatively evaluated by others is a signal for being potentially excluded from our social group. Therefore, social anxiety and fear of negative evaluation are adaptive (and good) if we experience it in situations when it makes sense to feel anxious. Regardless of whether it is adaptive or not, anxiety is always an unpleasant experience. For this reason, we want to avoid feeling anxious, even when it is helpful. After successfully avoiding anxiety, such as by leaving a party earlier than you'd planned or not going at all, you probably feel relief that you got out of this situation. You might feel glad that you were able to stop the suffering (in case you entered the situation and used anxiety-reducing strategies) or glad that you were able to successfully bail out of it (in case you decided not to enter the situation in the first place).

However, it is not the same kind of relief that one experiences when a pain is gone or after a difficult decision is made. It is a bittersweet feeling of relief. You might also feel sad, disappointed, angry at yourself, or frightened and worried about similar scenarios in the future. For example, if you left a party with close friends early, you may spend most of the next day ruminating about whether your friends missed you or had more fun without you, even though they invited you in the first place. Will you be able to avoid your anxiety again in the future? What if you can't use the same avoidance strategy the next time you encounter a similar situation? Or what if the strategy will not work as well as this time? As a result, people often feel even greater anxiety about a situation after they have successfully avoided similar situations in the past. Avoidance is an imperfect method to reduce maladaptive anxiety. It helps in the present moment by removing the distressing situation but makes it even more difficult in similar future situations. It teaches you that you can't deal with the distress of social anxiety, even though you can.

The relationship between anxiety and avoidance is illustrated in figure 3. This figure shows the two consequences of avoidance behaviors. The first one is relief. This is the immediate and short-term positive consequence of anxiety. However, there is also the long-term negative consequence of avoidance. That is, you will always feel anxious in this particular situation. In fact, you might even feel more anxious about a similar situation in the future, simply *because* you avoided it before. This heightened level of anxiety that you experience even before entering the situation is called *anticipatory anxiety*. If you have high anticipatory anxiety about a social situation, you most likely have used avoidance strategies in the past. For example, leaving the party early reduces your anxiety and is a form of avoidance. People often don't realize that they use avoidance strategies, even when they do. Identifying avoidance can be difficult. Because avoidance is smart—very smart—but we can outsmart it by disrupting the anxiety-avoidance cycle through prolonged and/or repeated exposure to the anxiety-producing situation.

Avoidance Is Just as Smart as You Are

"Hey, wanna join us for some drinks after work?" asks your coworker. The question comes out of nowhere and hits you like a bullet. You are so shocked that the only response you can think of is "Sure." You are panicking inside. "Great. We'll meet you downstairs in about five," your coworker replies with a smile. But as they are walking away, you hear yourself say, "Oh wait. I forgot that I need to finish the report that's due tomorrow. So sorry. Maybe next time."

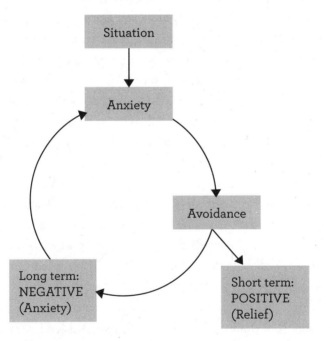

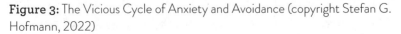

Figure 3: The Vicious Cycle of Anxiety and Avoidance (copyright Stefan G. Hofmann, 2022)

Your avoidance scored again. Next time, you will find another creative way to avoid. Remember, avoidance behaviors can be difficult to identify. This is because your avoidance is very smart. In fact, it is just as smart as you are. Maybe there is, in fact, a report you need to finish soon. There will always be a reason why you can't put yourself in a particular social situation. What is your favorite avoidance strategy? Here are some examples of what people do before or during a public speaking situation in order to reduce their anxiety:

- postponing or bailing out of the presentation for various reasons (e.g., *This is just not a good day; I don't feel good; I don't have time because I have to complete this other task first; My dog has diarrhea*)

- taking medications such as beta-blockers (propranolol or atenolol) beforehand

- preparing extensively (and excessively) for the presentation (e.g., studying the topic and related areas so thoroughly that you are prepared to answer any possible question)

- learning the speech by heart and having detailed written notes in front of you

- doing meditation and relaxation exercises before the talk

- carrying some peppermints with you

- dressing up

- wearing a special tie, shirt, shoes, etc.

- carrying your favorite pen

But look at yourself from an outsider's perspective for a minute and ask yourself: *What is the real function of these behaviors?* Do you show these behaviors regularly before or during social situations, and do you think they help reduce your anxiety? None of these reasons are completely irrational. They all make sense, because avoidance is just as smart as you are. Your avoidance will always find reasons why you should or shouldn't do something; some might be more convincing to you and other people than others. However, the bottom line is this: if you are struggling with social anxiety, that means you are avoiding the feeling of anxiety in some way. Period. And this is the most important reason why anxiety is so persistent. Here are some concrete examples of Sarah's avoidance strategies. (You can find a blank copy of this table at http://www.newharbinger.com/51208.)

Table 2: Sarah's Most Common Avoidance Strategies

Avoidance Strategy	How Often Do You Use It? (Almost never, sometimes, often, almost always, or always)
Overpreparing for a speech (like last week)	Always
Carrying peppermints with me	Always
Coming up with an excuse to avoid (like last week)	Almost always (when it's possible)
Drinking alcohol at social gatherings	Often
Doing relaxation exercises before the speech	Often
Carrying atenolol with me	Often
Taking atenolol	Sometimes
Not showing up at all	Almost never
Escaping the situation	Almost never

Sarah always overprepares for a speech unless she can avoid such situations altogether. She also developed a habit of having peppermints in her pocket when she has to give speeches in case her mouth gets too dry and her voice cracks. She also often does relaxation exercises before her speech. Her social anxiety is not limited to public speaking. Social gatherings are often anxiety provoking, too. If she has to go to social gatherings, she often drinks alcohol. Though the alcohol makes Sarah feel comfortable and she does not drink to excess, it still qualifies as an avoidance behavior because it keeps her from facing her social fear.

Sarah was excellent in identifying some of her subtle avoidance strategies. For example, she was able to realize that she prepared for a speech more than was really necessary. She did this to reduce her anxiety and therefore correctly classified it as an avoidance strategy. This example nicely illustrates that avoidance can be expressed in many different ways. Avoidance does not simply mean not entering a fearful situation. As you remember from our earlier discussion, we define avoidance very broadly as anything you do or don't do that keeps you from facing your fear. In Sarah's case, this included overpreparing for a speech (because she used it avoid facing her fear), carrying peppermints with her, and simply coming up with an excuse to avoid being confronted with the fearful situation.

All of these behaviors are avoidance strategies—some more subtle than others. The most obvious form of avoidance is not entering the feared situation in the first place (for various more or less plausible reasons). Other behaviors (or lack thereof) are more difficult to identify as avoidance behaviors. However, in each case, you do something (or don't do something) that keeps you from facing your fear. Some of those activities can be easily justified without even mentioning your anxiety. For example, you might say to yourself that you are just a person striving for perfection and therefore spend more time preparing, studying, and practicing for your presentation or public appearance than most people. Or you may say to yourself that you just like relaxation exercises because they are generally good for your health. Or you might tell yourself that you wear these special clothes to this presentation because you are a person with style. And the favorite pen brings you luck. Do you see how smart avoidance can be?

Avoidance Is Your Anxiety's Best Friend

Imagine that you are sitting in your office in front of your computer and are surfing the web. It's a slow morning, and you are a bit bored. Suddenly, your boss comes into your office and asks you to join her in the big conference room where a large group of people is gathered. Your boss wants you to give a presentation in front of this group about a project you were recently involved in. But you know fairly little about it. None of your other colleagues who have worked on this project are around. What would happen to your anxiety?

Let's assume that this situation would create intense anxiety, and you would give it a rating of 9 on a scale from 1 to 10 (see figure 4). You hate to disappoint your boss, but you decide to come up with an excuse and tell her that you won't be able to join her because you have to finish an important project. Your boss says, "Too bad" and leaves your office. What would happen to your anxiety after you avoided the presentation? It would probably go down very quickly and you would feel relief and probably some guilt. This is the short-term positive consequence. As a result, however, you will never know how bad the situation would have been and whether or not you could have handled it. Of course, you would also miss out on the opportunity to experience a positive outcome of the situation if you had impressed your colleagues and superiors, which could have advanced your career or led to new friendships. Therefore, similar situations in the future will create the same (if not more) anxiety. This is the long-term negative consequence of avoidance: avoidance will lead to the same (or even greater) anxiety if the situation repeats itself.

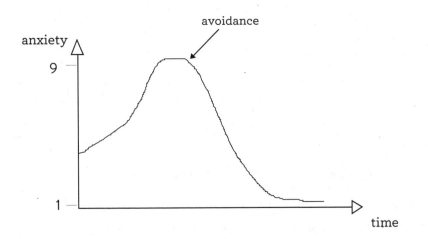

Figure 4: Time Course of Anxiety with Avoidance (copyright Stefan G. Hofmann, 2022)

How to Make It Stop

So far, we have discussed the reasons why social anxiety can persist for many years and why it can be so disabling and pervasive. The following sections will introduce you to the various strategies that can make it stop. As you'll remember from the previous chapter, anxiety consists of three components: behavior, bodily symptoms, and thoughts (figure 1). These components interact and feed on each other, which contributes to the pervasiveness of the problem. This is the bad news. The good news, however, is that this opens up a number of possibilities of how to change your social anxiety.

Letting Anxiety Go Down All by Itself

Now let's imagine a different scenario: Your boss comes into your office and asks you to give a presentation in front of a lot of people about a topic that you are not very familiar with. Instead of avoiding the situation, you enter the room. People stop talking. All eyes are on you. Everybody waits for you to say something. Your anxiety is now at an extremely high level (figure 5). Let's say you are now standing in front of all these people; everybody is looking at you, waiting for you to start your speech. You can feel your heart pounding, your palms sweating, et cetera. Let's assume that you had a time machine and could press the "pause button" and remain in that situation for a while. So let's press the "pause" button on our time machine. What would your anxiety be, say, after two minutes…what would it be after ten minutes…what would it be after one hour (our time machine is still on "pause")…what would your anxiety be after two hours…and what would it be after ten hours of just standing there with the audience looking at you in great expectation? As shown in figure 5, your anxiety will eventually decrease, because *anxiety will go down just by itself if you don't avoid it. No matter what.*

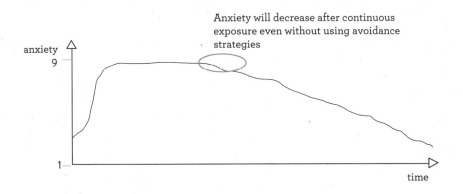

Figure 5: Time Course of Anxiety Without Avoidance (copyright Stefan G. Hofmann, 2022)

When comparing figure 4 with figure 5, it is obvious that it will take much longer for anxiety to go down if you didn't use any avoidance strategies. It might even stay at the maximum level for a very long period of time, and it may go up and down for some time before it gradually drops off. However, your anxiety will go down eventually, all by itself. This reduction in your anxiety response happens automatically and naturally. Your body has regulatory mechanisms that become active during repeated and continuous exposure to stress. In general, the term "stress" refers to reactions to events that we perceive as endangering our general well-being. It is important to note that it is our *perception* of an event—and not the event per se—that causes the stress response. For example, meeting the same new person can be enjoyable for some people but very anxiety provoking for others.

Scientists can observe and measure a number of typical psychological and physiological changes when a person perceives something as stressful. Psychological reactions to stress are often emotional responses ranging from exhilaration (when the event is demanding but manageable and pleasant) to anxiety, frustration, anger, and depression (when the event is perceived as uncontrollable). The physiological stress response is the result of a very complex sequence of biological mechanisms. Some of these responses are short lasting and resolve quickly, while others are long-lasting changes with the purpose of adapting to the continued presence of a stressor.

The short-lasting, emergency-type changes in response to stress are those of the fight-or-flight response (which we have already discussed). Our body is equipped with this system to prepare us to either fight or flee in the presence of danger (or better: perceived danger). When confronted with a stressor (such as a stressful event, task, situation, or object), our body needs energy. Therefore, the liver releases extra sugar to fuel the muscles. Stress hormones are released into our blood stream, activating our body's fight-or-flight response system. As a result, our heart rate, blood pressure, breathing rate, and muscle tension increase, our mouth gets dry, and the surface blood vessels constrict, among other things.

Most of these physiological changes result from the activation of our neuroendocrine system that is primarily controlled by the hypothalamus, a small structure located in the middle of our brain. One of the systems that are controlled by the hypothalamus is the sympathetic branch of our autonomic nervous system. This sympathetic nervous system then acts directly on our organs and muscles to produce increased heart rate, greater fluctuations in electrodermal activity, elevated blood pressure, and other changes. It also stimulates the release of adrenaline and cortisol into the blood stream; these hormones are often referred to as the "stress hormones." This leads to an increase in heart rate, blood pressure, and electrodermal activity, among other things.

After a certain amount of time, when the stressful (anxiety-producing) situation persists, our body starts to downregulate the level of arousal. The parasympathetic nervous system, one of the two branches of our autonomic nervous system, becomes more active, while the influence of the other branch, the sympathetic nervous system, decreases. As a result, our heart rate decreases, our breathing rate slows down, less blood is transported to the large muscle groups and the periphery, and so on. In other words, our body eventually habituates to the anxiety-provoking situation. But habituation is most effective when you experience your anxiety to its fullest. This means staying in the situation for an extended period of time without using any kind of avoidance strategies. The following conversation between Sarah and me (her therapist) is a good example:

Sarah: How is it that getting into our anxiety is going to help us when we've been suffering for a long time?

Therapist: Because every time we experience anxiety, our reaction is to try to make it go away. And that's bad because avoidance leads to the maintenance of anxiety. Anxiety could not exist without avoidance. Does this make sense?

Sarah: But how should we act when feeling anxious? Would I just psyche myself into an attitude where I say, "Great! I am feeling anxious. This is wonderful! My mouth is really dry. I can't think of what I want to talk about. I'm shaking, I'm blushing, I feel horrible, I want to run away." How can this help?

Therapist: Good point. What do you think? Why does repeated and prolonged exposure to fearful situations decrease anxiety in those situations? Has it ever happened to you?

Sarah: Yes. One of my girlfriends has been dragging me to the Zumba dance class. I really didn't want to do it, but I couldn't say no to her. She really wanted to do it with me. Although I did feel very anxious, it just kind of went away by itself.

Therapist: Excellent. Why did it go down?

Sarah: Don't know. I got used to it?

Therapist: Can you explain this a little more?

Sarah: Like you said, anxiety goes down on its own after a while.

Therapist: Right. As long as you avoid, you will continue to have this anxiety in this particular situation. And this is not only true for anxiety—as soon as you try to control your emotion, your emotion will control you. The only way to get rid of your anxiety is by accepting it—embrace it, bathe in it, welcome it, let it stay there if it wants to stay there. Eventually, it will go down. And the more often and the longer and the more intense you experience this in a particular situation, the less anxious you will feel in the future. And there is nothing that you need to do. Just experience your anxiety to its fullest; don't do anything to make it go away or diminish it. I am not saying that you need to learn how to enjoy the feeling of anxiety. Anxiety is a normal but very unpleasant experience. No one likes to feel anxious. This is why drug companies manufacture anxiety-reducing and not anxiety-inducing drugs—because they would probably not sell very well…

This example demonstrates the principle of exposure therapy: face your fear, and your fear will diminish. The decrease of your anxiety as a result of prolonged and repeated exposure is called habituation. As we discussed earlier, this occurs for a number of reasons. The main point here is that it works; anxiety *will* eventually go down if you don't avoid. It works for all species and all humans. There are no exceptions.

Teaching Your Body a New Habit

Let's assume you decided not to avoid your boss's request to join her in the conference room despite your apprehension. And let's also assume you could stay in the situation as long as you wanted (i.e., we would rewind the time machine and repeat the scene over and over again). What do you think would happen the next few times you encounter the same situation after you successfully exposed yourself to it the first time? As shown in figure 6, you will experience less anticipatory anxiety, a smaller maximum anxiety, and a quicker reduction in anxiety. The four curves in figure 6 represent four times you encounter the same situation. The top curve shows the typical anxiety response the first time you encounter the situation. This curve is identical to the curve in figure 5. The bottom curve is your anxiety after numerous times exposing yourself to the same situation without using any avoidance strategies. As your anxiety decreases with time, you will become more comfortable in the situation, which will also have a positive effect on your performance.

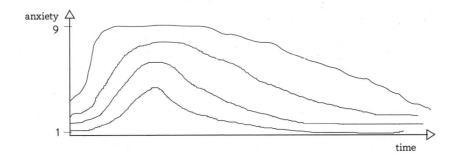

Figure 6: Anxiety After Repeated Exposures to the Same Situation (copyright Stefan G. Hofmann, 2022)

Habituation is a learning process. Like any learning process, it takes time, but it will get easier and easier the more often you do it and the more you realize that (a) the feared outcome is not going to happen and (b) if it does happen, you can cope with it. Unfortunately, this learning process can be very painful because it requires you to stay in the situation and endure a great deal of discomfort for a lengthy period of time. However, there is a payoff: Your anxiety will eventually decrease. You'll learn that you can tolerate not just the anxiety, but the thing that makes you anxious. And the more often you expose yourself to the same situation without using any avoidance strategies, the less anxiety you will experience in the future.

The hard thing to accept is that only repeated and prolonged exposure leads to habituation. A single brief exposure won't do the trick. You need to do it for long enough and/or often enough that you get used to the situation, which eventually decreases your anxiety. If you feel that things can't get much worse, just keep on going; there is light at the end of the tunnel. This requires from you a leap in faith and a great deal of courage; you are courageous because you confront a situation despite your fear. Remember that avoidance is broadly defined as anything you do or don't do that keeps you from facing your fear. This often develops into a habit, and habits are hard to identify and hard to break. Also, remember that avoidance is as intelligent as you are and often gives you other reasons why you don't want to do something. Your avoidance will always find reasons why you shouldn't or can't do it right now, some of which are more convincing to you and other people than others. But the bottom line is: you are avoiding. Period.

Making an Informed Decision

Avoidance is a choice. Not avoiding is a choice. Both choices have consequences. Remember the short-term and long-term consequences of avoidance? (Please take another look at figure 3). The short-term consequence of avoidance is relief, and the long-term consequence is the maintenance of your anxiety. In contrast, the short-term consequence of exposure is distress, and its long-term consequence is the elimination of your anxiety. Thus, both avoidance and exposure lead to short-term and long-term consequences. However, only the long-term negative consequence of avoidance is the reason for your problem. The different consequences of exposure and avoidance are summarized in table 3.

Table 3: Short-Term and Long-Term Consequences of
Avoidance and Exposure
(Copyright Stefan G. Hofmann)

	Short-Term Consequence	Long-Term Consequence
Avoidance	Relief	Maintenance of anxiety
Exposure	Distress	Elimination of anxiety

It is completely up to you to decide how to respond to your anxiety. The quick and easy way to deal with it (by avoiding it) leads to the maintenance, and often worsening, of the problem. In contrast, doing it the hard way (by exposing yourself) is very difficult at first but gets easier and easier with time and eventually leads to the elimination of your anxiety. If you avoid, anxiety controls you. But if you expose yourself, you take the first step toward controlling your anxiety.

Linguistics and communication scientists like to say that it is impossible not to communicate. As soon as you put two people together in one room, there will always be some sort of communication going on: some messages are being delivered verbally, others nonverbally through facial expressions and gestures, or the lack thereof. If you keep getting a nasty email from somebody and you decide not to respond, although you usually respond to your emails right away, this conveys the message "I am just going to ignore you (you bastard)." When you start ignoring your four-year-old son who asks you repeatedly, "Can I have some ice cream" after you clearly told him no numerous times, you may be conveying the message "Be quiet now or Daddy will get mad." The action, or lack thereof, can carry many different meanings and can only be understood by knowing the intention and the context of the situation. Interestingly, the decision not to respond to a question or provocation can carry as much meaning as responding to it directly.

Being confronted with a fear-provoking situation can also be considered a provocation. Similarly, if you think avoidance simply means putting something off for later, think again. Every time you avoid, you communicate to yourself and other people that anxiety is stronger than you. Every time you avoid, you are making a decision against an independent and anxiety-free life and for a life that is controlled by your anxiety. And every time you don't avoid, you are courageous and choose the hard way with the goal to free yourself from your anxiety in the future. You can compare it to a baseball game: Every time you avoid, your anxiety (the other team) scores. This means that you will have to try a lot harder in the inning. The more you avoid, the more difficult it will become to win the game. In other words, avoidance does not simply mean putting a decision off. Rather, it means making a decision for your anxiety and against an independent life.

So make this a priority for the upcoming weeks as you are working through this book. Nothing should be more important than dealing with your social anxiety for now. Nothing. Not even your dog's diarrhea. You can gain a lot, but you have little to lose. The new approach toward your anxiety won't just make you feel more comfortable in social performance situations. It is much more than that; it entails a change in lifestyle. Clearly saying no to avoidance also means choosing the hard way with the goal to live a better life in the future—a life without anxiety. This applies to virtually all areas in your life. So the next time you avoid, be aware that at the same time you are making a decision for a life that is controlled by your anxiety, and against an anxiety-free life.

Your avoidance may soon whisper into your ear: "Don't listen to this book; don't do the exposure exercises; it is not going to work." In this case, tell your avoidance to shut up and that you will do it anyway because you never know unless you try it. Give it a shot. You don't have anything to lose but your avoidance and your anxiety.

Real Exposure Is the Best Exposure

The most effective exposures are real-life exposures. Nothing beats the real situation. But exposures to things that approximate real life can also be quite helpful. Rehearsing a speech in front of a mirror or in front of your dog or cat is better than nothing. If you can convince your friend to serve as an audience, even better. There are many companies that specialize in virtual reality that allow users to do virtual reality exposures. During virtual reality exposures, you wear a headset, and a computer displays a virtual scene with a feared situation, such as a classroom. This can be beneficial, especially as initial steps toward the real deal. If you do virtual exposure, make sure you create a situation that elicits anxiety and then confront your anxiety head on, without using any avoidance strategies to lessen your fear. Another modification is "imaginal exposure," repeated exposure to a fearful image. Here is an example. Please read the following paragraph and picture the scene as vividly as possible:

> You have to give a presentation in front of a big class. Everybody is looking at you, waiting for you to begin your speech. You feel intense panic as you are facing the audience. Your mouth is dry. You feel very hot and your face is flushed. The palms of your hands are cold and sweaty. Your heart is pounding fast and loudly. You feel light-headed and dizzy. You feel overwhelmed by negative thoughts as you are facing the audience.

Now close your eyes and picture this scene as vividly as you can for a few minutes.

You probably experienced some feelings of discomfort as you were imagining this situation. We know that imagining a fearful situation creates very similar, although less intense, reactions than being in the real situation. People differ in their ability to imagine a scene vividly. The more vivid the imagined scene is, the closer it feels to reality.

Psychologists use the principle of imaginal exposure by asking patients to repeatedly picture a fearful scene as vividly as possible. These exposures can then provide you with a chance to practice a number of strategies we will describe in more detail later.

Exposures Test Your Assumptions

Exposing yourself to a feared situation gives you the opportunity to test your beliefs and see if the feared consequence actually occurs. Because you have been avoiding experiencing your anxiety to its fullest in those situations, you have never given yourself the chance to see what actually happens. Exposure works not only because you habituate, but because it provides you with an opportunity to test your beliefs and examine the actual "danger" of the situation. As long as you avoid talking to your coworker because you are afraid of getting rejected, you will never know if the person will actually reject you!

Only exposure to the situation will tell you whether the situation is indeed as bad as you expect it to be, and, in case it actually is that bad, whether you have ways to cope with it. So even if your coworker will reject you—so what? Sure, it will be unpleasant, but life will go on. There are many people in this world who would love to talk to you and not reject you. Thus, exposure provides you with the opportunity to test some of your negative predictions and make you realize that nothing is going to happen. In order for exposure to work, you have to experience repeated and prolonged anxiety to its fullest, put your negative thoughts to the test, and take a leap of faith. You never know unless you try it. I have a lot more to say about this later.

Repeated and prolonged exposure will make you realize that your social skills are not nearly as bad as you initially thought they were, which will also increase your self-confidence. As you start learning news ways of coping with the situation and your anxiety, your sense of control over your emotions and the situation will also increase. It is a well-known fact that lack of control leads to distress. Furthermore, it has been demonstrated that repeated experience with uncontrollable and unpleasant situations can lead to anxiety and depression. Conversely, an increased sense of control enhances your mood and your self-confidence. If you repeatedly avoid your anxiety in social situations, you will perceive the situation as being out of your control and will believe the only way to control it is to avoid it (which is the worst coping strategy for the reasons we discussed above). By exposing yourself to the fearful situation, you will learn ways to cope with your anxiety that you haven't known before.

One reason why exposure works for you and others with social anxiety is because you learn that your social skills are not nearly as bad as you thought they were (in fact, you may realize that they are actually quite good)—in other words, your self-efficacy increases. It is therefore important to receive some (honest) feedback about your social performance so that you can evaluate your own social skills. Most likely, there will be very little, if anything, that needs to be improved.

In conclusion, I outlined in this chapter why exposure is such a key strategy to overcome debilitating social anxiety. You learned that anxiety per se is actually not the primary problem; it's the avoidance, and that's what we need to target. Anxiety couldn't persist if you didn't avoid. We defined avoidance as anything you do or don't do that keeps you from facing your fear. Some avoidance is obvious, while other forms of avoidance are subtle and hard to catch. It is smart (as smart as you are), but once we catch it, we can fight it and eliminate it. Avoidance causes relief in the short term, but it has disastrous consequences in the long term. If you avoid fearful situations, you experience relief from your anxiety in the short term, but in the long term, your avoidance is responsible for maintaining your anxiety. Therefore, avoidance is your anxiety's best friend, and your anxiety only persists because you avoid. This also means that the most effective way to deal with your anxiety is to fight the avoidance, and you can eliminate avoidance through repeated and/or prolonged exposures. These exposure practices are not pleasant. But they are the only way to effectively reduce and eventually eliminate your social anxiety in the long term. The beauty of repeated and prolonged exposure to the fearful situation is that these changes are not only limited to the target exposure situations (e.g., becoming more comfortable when giving a speech in the Wednesday meeting); they are not even limited to only a specific type of situation (public speaking situations). Instead, the changes typically generalize to a number of fearful social situations (e.g., giving a toast at a dinner party, dating, participating in meetings). As a result, repeated exposures broaden and expand your life. Through exposure, you invest some short-term pain in order to gain your long-term freedom.

CHAPTER 4

Identifying and Correcting Thinking Errors

I am such an idiot. I will make a fool of myself. I stink. How are you feeling as you are reading these words? Not good, right? Thinking these words to yourself as you are standing in front of an audience or having dinner with somebody will feel even worse. The way we think has an enormously powerful influence on our emotional response. Our thoughts are the filters of the world. In fact, it is not the situation per se, but rather our perceptions, expectations, and interpretations of events that are responsible for our emotions. Let's say you see your neighbor on the street. You look into her eyes and quietly greet her. But she doesn't respond and just walks by you. There are different ways to interpret this situation, leading to different emotional responses. Perhaps you think she didn't notice you and you might find her inattentiveness amusing; perhaps you think she is upset or angry with you, which might cause you to be worried; or perhaps you think she ignores you because she doesn't like you, which would make you feel hurt. Different feelings arise depending on the way you interpret the same situation.

The tools you learn in this chapter will teach you how to identify and correct some of the thinking patterns that maintain your social anxiety. These tools are effective for targeting a number of cognitive aspects supporting your social anxiety, also referred to as maintaining factors (see chapter 2, figure 2: Maintenance of SAD). This includes your tendency to focus your attention inwardly, which may lead you to notice aspects about yourself that you don't like when you're in a social situation. You'll learn strategies to change this negative view of yourself and become comfortable with the way you are, and you'll realize that other people do not share the same negative view as you. The thinking tools you'll learn will also target your belief that social mishaps have disastrous consequences for you. They do not. Finally, the thinking tools will help you stop ruminating about past social encounters—not only on the negative aspects, but also on ambiguous aspects (things that could be interpreted as negative or positive), which you may tend to interpret negatively. Again, this does not help and makes the situation much worse. There is a lot to cover in this chapter. So let's get started.

Epictetus, one of the ancient Greek philosophers, summarized this observation in the statement: "Men are not moved by things but the views which they take of them." In other words, we are only anxious, angry, or sad if we think that we have reason to be anxious, angry, or sad. The Roman emperor (and Stoic philosopher) Markus Aurelius (121–180 CE) said, "If you are distressed by anything external, the pain isn't due to the thing itself, but to your estimate of it, and this you have the power to revoke at any moment." By "estimate," he meant interpretation, which, as we discussed earlier, can influence the pain or anxious distress we experience. But Markus Aurelius took it a step further by saying that we have the ability to reject the interpretations we make. This means we can do something about our thinking. We have the ability to slow down and become aware of our automatic thoughts, and then evaluate whether they're realistic.

Because thinking can be automatic and you've been thinking in the same way for a long time, these skills can initially be difficult to learn. Learning to observe your thinking is a skill that requires patience and practice. In the beginning, it will be hard to slow down and watch your thinking, but keep working at it. You're not alone! Remember, you can use your *feelings* of anxiety as a signal that there may be automatic, irrational, anxious thoughts under the surface that need to be examined. Thoughts about some possible bad outcome are a major component of feeling anxious and often drive anxiety-related physical sensations and behaviors. So, even if you're not aware of exactly what the thoughts are, use your feelings as an indicator that it's time to slow down and pay attention to your thoughts. If you do this consistently, you'll start to notice more patterns and your automatic thoughts will become easier to detect.

Automatic thoughts are like habits, and habits are hard to break. Think about it this way: If you've spent years thinking that people don't like to be around you, it will take work to realize that some people actually do like to be around you. But first, you will have to become aware of these automatic patterns, test them to see if they are true, change them if necessary, and then develop alternative, more adaptive patterns. For example, if you always avoid going to parties, start asking yourself why that is and what you are concerned about. If you think it's because you believe nobody will want to talk to you, test it out and start going to parties. If you have gone to a number of parties and nobody has talked to you, you know that you were right. But if that didn't happen (and I bet that's the case), it's time to replace the old (bad) habit with a new (good) habit, which means that you should start going to parties to talk to people! We will say more about the nature of automatic thoughts later.

The late Aaron T. Beck, a renowned psychiatrist and professor at the University of Pennsylvania, adopted this principle to treat emotional disorders, including SAD (Beck and Emery 1985). The resulting technique, cognitive behavioral therapy (CBT), has become the most influential contemporary treatment approach. CBT was first successfully applied to the treatment of depression and then expanded to virtually all mental disorders (Hofmann et al. 2012). A CBT model for SAD was first developed and systematically tested by Richard Heimberg, Debra Hope, Ronald Rapee and their colleagues (Heimberg et al. 1990; Rapee and Heimberg 1997). Many of the principles described in this book would not have been possible without the groundbreaking and pioneering work of these investigators.

The word "cognitive" in cognitive behavioral therapy implies that treatment mainly concentrates on thought processes. However, CBT does not mean that therapy is limited to modification of our thoughts, or cognitions. It simply means that the therapist gets to the client's emotions through cognitions. The client's emotional and behavioral responses are of equal importance. Effective CBT targets all aspects of an emotional disorder, including emotional experience, behavior, and cognitions. Specifically, CBT includes an intellectual, an experiential, and a behavioral approach, all of which are important aspects in therapy. As part of the *intellectual* approach, you learn to identify you misconceptions, test the validity of your thoughts, and substitute them with more appropriate concepts. The *experiential* approach exposes you to the experiences in order to change your misconceptions. The central element of the *behavioral* approach is the development of specific forms of behavior that lead to more general changes in the way you view yourself and the world.

To briefly illustrate the technique as it applies to SAD, let's go back to our scenario where your boss asked you to give a speech in front of a large group of people about a subject matter you are not very familiar with. Some thoughts might come to mind that make you very anxious (e.g., *I have to give a perfect talk and should not show any anxiety. Otherwise my boss will be very angry at me*). Other thoughts may actually lead to a decrease of your anxiety (e.g., *Everyone gets nervous before these presentations. I can make a few mistakes and the talk can still go well; people may not even notice my anxiety*). In one case, your anxiety can easily get out of control, and in the other case your thoughts can actually calm you down. Depending on how you feel and what you think, your behavior will also be different. Anxious thoughts will make you want to avoid, non-anxious thoughts will make you motivated. Thus, your thoughts directly cause your emotions and your behaviors. Of course, your behavior will also influence your thoughts and your feelings, and your feelings will also influence your thoughts and your behaviors.

Automatic Thoughts

Thoughts serve a vital purpose—they help us evaluate situations, make quick judgments, form potential solutions, and consider what might happen if we act a certain way. In fact, we're so dependent on thinking that sometimes we're hardly aware we're doing it! This is what we mean when we refer to *automatic thinking*. Cognitive therapists call these thoughts "automatic" because they may occur without (or with little) conscious awareness. These automatic thoughts often lead to distortion of reality because they create a misperception, or exaggeration, of the situation.

Automatic thinking happens quickly. There is a reason for this: being able to think quickly is adaptive. You make hundreds of decisions in any given day, including what to eat, what to wear, how to get to work or school, what projects to work on at your job, what music to listen to, what to watch on TV, what time to go to bed… You get the idea. That's a lot of information for your brain to sort through! If the process of thinking were deliberate and slow, it would take us too long to assess a situation and determine our course of action. Much of the time, automatic thinking works very well for us. It's less effortful for our brain and lets us evaluate social situations, form quick judgments, and make efficient decisions.

However, sometimes automatic thinking creates unintended problems. Namely, our brain develops shortcuts that lead to errors and irrational conclusions. An example is the neighbor you see on the street who seems to ignore you or didn't see you. In the first case you jump to the conclusion "she doesn't like me," and in the second case, you think she is inattentive. These mental shortcuts allow us to think efficiently, but they're prone to bias and contribute to things like stereotypes and prejudice. Imagine you have to buy a birthday gift for your friend's five-year-old daughter and you assume she'd like a doll rather than a toy car. Although this may be a relatively benign example, stereotypes can sometimes be harmful because they're overgeneralized assumptions. In the same way, mental shortcuts can contribute to biases in thinking that lead to problematic anxiety.

Thinking Errors

We know there are no guarantees that every situation you face will be successful. In fact, providing positive but unfounded self-talk (*I'm sure that my talk will be great*) may only serve to increase pressure and provide unrealistic standards for performance. This type of self-talk can be just as inaccurate as the negative cognitions that are more typical of anxious individuals. The goal is not to think positively all the time but to be more realistic and accurate in your appraisals of your abilities as well as the actual threat presented by the situations you face.

Negative predictions are common in individuals with other anxiety problems. Unhelpful thoughts, known as maladaptive cognitions, associated with anxiety disorders tend to be future-oriented perceptions of danger or threat (e.g., *What is about to happen?*). If you have SAD, the focus is usually on the consequence of public scrutiny and subsequent negative evaluation (*Nobody is going to like me, I'm going to make a fool of myself*) and on a sense of uncontrollability over the situation or symptoms of anxiety. Another hallmark of anxious cognitions is that they tend to be automatic or habitual, such that you put no effort into conjuring up such thoughts. Instead, they often occur instantaneously and sometimes in response to subtle cues.

The goal here is not to think *positively* but rather to think more *realistically* and *adaptively*. Adaptive thinking not only gives you a more realistic perspective, but it also guides you toward coping strategies to deal with the situation at hand. If a situation is really very bad, and you have good reason to feel bad, then you should feel bad unless you refuse to face reality. For example, the loss of a loved one, a serious personal financial crisis, and serious health problems are all good reasons to feel bad, stressed, anxious, and sad. But although giving a bad speech in front of colleagues might be an unpleasant and embarrassing event, it is no catastrophe. Compared to real catastrophes, it is really no big deal. Plus, in most cases you will perceive your own social performance much more negatively than other people will. For example, some people might assume you are tired because they think that you are a good speaker in general. Thus, the actual situation may not even be so bad, but it is your appraisal of the situation that makes you feel bad for no good reason. In order to know how realistic your thoughts, perception, and expectations about the situation really are, you will need to test your predictions. If your boss or the audience is really as hostile as you initially expected, you have good reason to avoid the scenario next time around. But if not, your worry is unrealistic and maladaptive.

We often have great difficulty identifying our thoughts, either because they are so much a part of our personality or because they occur without our being consciously aware of it. Thinking errors are dysfunctional beliefs or negative automatic thoughts. Dysfunctional (or irrational, maladaptive) beliefs are basic assumptions we have about the world, the future, and ourselves. These global overarching beliefs provide a schema, which determines how we interpret a specific situation. For example, you may believe that you should always be entertaining, intelligent, and funny; that unless everyone likes you, you are worthless; or that you need to have the perfect answers ready for every question after you give a presentation.

Cognitive therapists call these thoughts *dysfunctional beliefs* because they lead to a biased and flawed perception of the situation. Such dysfunctional beliefs can cause you not only to be very anxious about public speaking situations, but also to feel depressed and apprehensive in a number of other situations. As a result, you may avoid interpersonal contact due to your anxiety about criticism, disapproval, and rejection and may feel inferior to others or inhibited in new interpersonal situations because of feelings of inadequacy. Such beliefs get you into trouble because you set unrealistic goals for yourself. These dysfunctional beliefs give rise to negative automatic thoughts or images that occur in specific situations when you feel anxious. These thoughts are the specific expressions of your dysfunctional beliefs. For example, you may think, *Other people will think I'm boring* or *I will embarrass myself* or *Other people will think I'm stupid* when facing the audience. The specific automatic thought "Other people will think I'm boring" is anxiety provoking if you hold the belief that you will be rejected by other people unless you are entertaining. Below are a number of rather typical automatic thinking errors (adapted from Burns 2020).

- **Emotional Reasoning:** Sometimes we treat thoughts that "feel" threatening to us as accurate, hard-and-fast truths. In fact, our brains are hardwired to take threatening information seriously, because ignoring it could endanger our survival. Analyzing our way through situations based on *feelings* rather than *facts* is referred to as *emotional reasoning.* When you engage in emotional reasoning, you make an incorrect inference based on how you feel. For example, you may think that everybody in the audience must perceive you as being incompetent and pitiful because *you feel* so incompetent and pitiful.

- **Black-and-White Thinking:** Few things in life are always good or always bad. It really depends on context. Although the reality consists of different shades of gray, you see it as either black (bad) or white (good) with no shades of gray. If your performance is not quite perfect, you see yourself as a total failure. For example, if one person in the audience yawns, you conclude that everybody is bored to death by your speech. Unless things go perfectly well, you conclude that things went perfectly wrong.

- **Personalization:** You take negative social events personally. For example, you may be convinced that the person in the audience who is yawning thinks you are the most boring speaker in the world, even though they might be yawning because they didn't get enough sleep last night.

- **Focusing on Negatives:** You pick out a single negative detail and ignore any positive aspects. As a result, your perception of reality becomes darkened, like the drop of ink that discolors an entire bucket of water. For example, even if many people in the audience are very attentive and interested, you still think that you are the most boring speaker in the world because one person fell asleep.

- **Disqualifying the Positives:** If there is no negative outcome and the situation actually went pretty well, you may simply discount the positives. For example, you may insist that you were only able to perform pretty well because the task was so easy, or because you were just lucky that day, or because this particular audience was just very nice. But you dismiss any explanation that would attribute the success to your own ability or effort.

- **Jumping to Conclusions:** You make a negative interpretation of an event even though you don't have any good evidence to support this. For example, you anticipate that your presentation will be a disaster, and you feel convinced that this prediction is an already established fact. This is also called a "fortune-teller error." You might also conclude that someone is reacting negatively toward you even though there is no clear evidence to make this assumption. For example, you might conclude for no good reason that people don't like you, or that they think you are incompetent, boring, and so on. This is also referred to as the "mind reading error."

- **Overgeneralization:** You get all worked up because you see a single negative event as a never-ending pattern. For example, one bad presentation does not mean that you are a bad speaker and should choose a different career. A breakup from a relationship does not mean that you are unable to maintain a friendship; one rejection does not mean that you are unlovable.

- **Catastrophizing:** Similarly, in catastrophizing you make a big deal out of something that is not a big deal and blow things out of proportion. For example, you may think that just because you mess up a particular presentation at work, your boss is going to fire you and then you would never be able to find another job, be unable to pay your mortgage, get divorced from your wife, and end up on the street, spending the rest of your life looking through trash cans.

Monitoring Thoughts to Bring Them into Awareness

The most effective way to bring negative automatic thoughts into conscious awareness is to pay close attention to them when they are likely to occur. The easiest way to do this is to monitor your thoughts before and after an anxiety-provoking social situation. Try to closely monitor any fearful social situations that you encounter during the day and your thoughts related to them. Once you have identified your automatic thoughts, you will need to come up with "tests" to determine whether or not these concerns are reasonable. If they are "unreasonable" (because they do not reflect reality), you might want to change them and adopt a more realistic appraisal of social situations. We will come to this later.

Let's follow Sarah through a particularly terrifying day. At 9 a.m. she had to give a presentation at her PTA meeting. Her anxiety was already at a 50 on a 0–100-point scale. She thought to herself *If I mess things up, they will think I am incompetent, and this will affect my son's education.* This is a good example of *catastrophizing* because she is blowing something unpleasant (messing up a speech) out of proportion (because it is highly unlikely that this would affect her son's education). To ensure that this wouldn't happen, she prepared her speech the day before and wrote it down (we call this a form of avoidance because it is a strategy intended to lower anxiety).

She was scheduled to go to a lunch party at work at noon. Because she was terrified of it, she came up with an excuse not to go. This overt avoidance brought her anxiety down to 20. Reflecting back, she felt uncomfortable because she thought people would probably notice her absence, which is an example of emotional reasoning (*I feel anxious, therefore the situation must be dangerous*).

In the afternoon, she had to give a presentation to the new trainees at work. As she had done for her PTA meeting, she had prepared excessively the night before, but her anxiety was still high (70 on a 0–100-point scale) during her presentation. Therefore, she decided to stop to bring her anxiety down. As a reason, she told her trainees that they would have a break. She thought, *If my presentation is not perfect, they will think I'm inadequate, which will negatively affect our working relationship* (an example of catastrophizing and jumping to conclusions) and *I am a total loser* (an example of black-and-white thinking). She also thought, *The presentation was a total disaster* (an example of disqualifying the positives) and *I am not cut out for this job; I am just a very bad speaker* (an example of overgeneralization). At the end of the day, she was exhausted. Even worse, she felt so low and down on herself. She even felt disgusted about herself. How pathetic! She just wanted to crawl into a hole and disappear. These examples show you that the way you think and act has a huge impact on your feelings and your sense of self (i.e., the way you view yourself). It can make you feel miserable. But it works both ways. There is also a way to get out of your hole and rise up.

Maladaptive Thinking Styles

Let's dig a little deeper into maladaptive thinking. Did you notice a pattern in these thinking errors? All of these errors are due to one or both thinking styles that you learned about before: *probability overestimation* (i.e., overestimating the likelihood of an unpleasant event) and *catastrophic thinking* (i.e., blowing an unpleasant event out of proportion). For example, people with SAD tend to believe that there is a high probability they are in danger of behaving in an inept and unacceptable fashion and that those behaviors will certainly lead to disastrous consequences in terms of loss of status, loss of worth, and social rejection. In other words, people with SAD overestimate the probability of an unpleasant event (that they behave inappropriately) and blow things out of proportion even if they did behave inappropriately. You can identify these thinking styles by asking yourself the following questions:

1. **What evidence do I have that the belief is true?** For example, Sarah was concerned that she'd mess up her speech during her morning meeting and that people would think she is incompetent, which would then affect her son's education. The evidence that her speech performance has anything to do with her son's education is slim to none.

2. **Based on my past experience, how often did this feared outcome actually happen?** Sarah gave many speeches in similar situations before. It's not clear what "messing up a speech" exactly means to her. But let's assume that it means stuttering and stammering some incoherent sentences. It wouldn't be the first time and nothing horrible happened.

3. **What is the worst that could happen?** The worst that could happen is that people listen to a bad speech (if they pay attention). But the world is still turning. People mess up a lot. But people forgive and forget.

4. **If this worst outcome happens, would I be able to cope with it?** No matter how bad something turns out to be, people are remarkably resilient. We usually underestimate how resourceful we are, and we seem to be unaware of our coping skills to deal with things. Bad things are unlikely to happen. And even if they do happen, we usually find a way to deal with them. And life goes on.

The first two questions identify errors in thinking associated with probability overestimation. People commit cognitive errors leading to probability overestimations if they believe that an unlikely and unpleasant event (such as losing a job, losing a friend, getting divorced) is likely to occur based on ambiguous clues. An example might be the employee who worries that a bad speech in front of her coworkers would risk the relationship with them, and that her coworkers would think that she is incompetent. She might further worry that, as a result, she would be asked to leave her company and be unable to find another job because of her bad reputation.

Questions three and four identify catastrophic thinking errors. These are errors that occur if an unpleasant event is in fact happening but the negative aspects of this event are greatly exaggerated and blown out of proportion. Typical examples of this thinking style might be *This is the worst thing that could have happened to me. I will have to quit my job and will end up with no money and no friends.*

If you are a person with anxiety, you probably commit thinking errors leading to probability overestimations rather frequently. For example, imagine that you arrange with your partner to meet you at home at a certain time, say at 5:30. You are waiting at home, and the clock turns to 6:30. Your partner is late. There are a number of possible reasons why your partner might be late. He might be stuck in traffic, or had to stay a bit longer at work, or... he got in a horrible car accident and is somewhere on the side of the road, bleeding to death. The latter possibility is an example of a probability overestimation: it is an unlikely and very unpleasant event that causes you enormous distress.

Let's take another example. Imagine you are home alone. It's the end of a long day, and you are ready to relax. Your roommate is away for the evening and not expected back anytime soon. You've just finished eating dinner and are sitting down to watch a movie. Suddenly you hear a door slam (adapted from Beck 1976). What goes through your mind in this exact moment? What do you *automatically think* in this very situation? Maybe your roommate came home early, which might make you feel concerned or surprised. Maybe someone broke into the house, which would likely cause fear. Maybe the wind blew the door shut, which might leave you unconcerned. As you can see, you could have several emotional responses to this situation depending on what you were thinking. This situation is inherently ambiguous, as are many situations in life. Thus, how you *feel* about a situation will depend on what you think and what conclusions you draw. If you had been watching a scary movie when this happened, you would be more likely to jump to the conclusion that somebody broke into the house. Thus, context matters and influences your automatic response. When people experience chronic problematic anxiety and physical tension, they're more likely to *think* in anxious ways. Because their body is in a constant state of tension and anxiety, they're more likely to produce anxious thoughts in response to ambiguous situations. This is because when the body is in a physically tense state, it's sending feedback to the brain that something is wrong. Being chronically anxious and tense *increases the likelihood* of having anxious thoughts.

Let's delve into these two major thinking styles more deeply.

Probability Overestimation

Probability overestimation is a common thinking error for people with various forms of anxiety, including social anxiety. As a reminder, probability overestimation means that you are making inaccurate or unreasonable predictions that an unlikely event is highly probable. People who fall into this trap exaggerate the likelihood that a bad outcome will happen. You can counter probability overestimation by considering the evidence for and against an anxious thought, estimating the actual odds that a negative outcome will occur, and generating alternative explanations and more probable possibilities.

A common example of probability overestimation is the fear of getting on an airplane because the plane might crash. For people who experience this type of fear, the likelihood of a crash may feel quite high. However, air travel is one of the safest modes of transportation. In the last ten years, there have been approximately 300 plane crashes on commercial passenger flights based on my internet research. This may seem high, but there are an estimated 100,000 flights *per day*, or 3.5 million flights *per year*. Thus, the probability of a plane crash over the past ten years was roughly 0.0000004, or less than one in a million. In contrast, 1 of every 2,500 people die of choking every year. So statistically, dining out should be much more terrifying than boarding an airplane. You can see where this is going: although an airplane crash is *possible*, it's extremely unlikely.

The same is true for many social threats. The probability of a really bad outcome is not impossible, it is often just not very likely. Social situations are considerably more complex than plane rides, and it is a lot easier to determine if the bad outcome actually did happen after a plane ride than after a speech. If the plane didn't crash, your prediction is 100% wrong. But how can you determine if you messed up a speech, for example? And, in Sarah's case, if she really did mess it up, how can she determine whether or not this affected her son's education? Here, the idea of *believability* of a thought is more appropriate than the likelihood of whether or not an event occurred. Believability captures likelihood, but it's more than that. It also allows you to step outside your mind and critically evaluate how likely, realistic, and plausible it is that an event will occur.

To sum up, countering anxious thoughts is *not* the same as "positive thinking" or replacing "bad" thoughts with "good" ones. In fact, the purpose of this exercise is *not* to generate biased thoughts in the other direction. Instead, the goal is to look at the evidence for and against an automatic thought and then come up with more *realistic* and *adaptive* alternatives.

Challenging Probability Overestimation

To counter probability overestimation, you'll need to slow down and critically examine your judgment by considering all available facts and possibilities. This can help you avoid jumping to conclusions or making overly broad generalizations. Considering other possibilities and evaluating the evidence is critical because judgments and predictions based on emotional reasoning are very likely to be biased.

Following are five concrete steps to counter probability overestimation. When going through these steps, you may find that some of the initial steps are more or less useful, or even become redundant, for certain thoughts. If that happens, then do what works best for you.

Step 1: Slow down and notice. The first step is slowing things down and noticing what's going on in your head. Automatic thoughts are very quick responses to things happening to you, and you tend to only focus on some aspects of a situation while ignoring many others. Once you give yourself some time to notice and observe your thoughts, you are able to see the entire picture that reflects reality more accurately.

If a thought makes you anxious, you must believe on some level that there is reason to feel anxious, and you interpret a situation as a threat. But thoughts are assumptions about reality; they are not the same as reality. So once you've observed your thought, write it down. Put the thought into words, even if the words only approximate your thought. Sometimes thoughts are not verbal statements but images and are hard to describe. Still, give it a shot and try to clarify the thoughts with words. For example, Sara wrote down the thought she had during a PTA meeting: *If I mess things up, they will think I am incompetent and this will affect my son's education.* She correctly labeled this catastrophizing because she is exaggerating the potential danger of this meeting to her son's education.

Once you identify a thought, consider how much do you actually believe the thought. If a thought seems to come very close to reality, it is more believable. In contrast, if a thought does not seem to match reality, it is not believable. For example, the thought that people in the audience dislike you so much that they will throw things at you might be very anxiety producing, but it does not seem very believable.

To determine the believability of a thought, ask yourself, *How believable is this thought on a scale of 0* (not at all believable) *to 100* (completely believable, absolutely true)? In the beginning, especially in more anxious moments, it's likely that you'll rate your thought as being highly believable (between 75 to 100), but as you reflect on it, its believability might decrease. This is quite normal. We tend to treat thoughts as facts even though they are simply assumptions. The believability rating will clarify this difference.

Step 2: Examine the evidence *for* and *against* the assumption. Now let's begin to examine the validity of the thought. This will help you think more rationally and less emotionally. Evidence is based on facts and objective information you could present to a judge in court, rather than baseless opinions. Examining evidence for versus against an assumption that seems like a natural conclusion requires a good degree of flexibility. This can be achieved by viewing things from another point of view. For example, put yourself in an independent observer's perspective. How would another person, not involved in the social interaction, view the interaction?

This can be challenging because it requires considering alternative ideas that are not as natural or automatic. We are naturally prone to seek information that supports our beliefs and ignore, or discount, information that goes against them. This phenomenon is called *confirmation bias*. This is especially the case when we're experiencing problematic anxiety. Stay with it though, and be patient with yourself, especially in the beginning. Getting the perspective of someone else can help you generate more objective evidence.

Step 3: Explore alternative possibilities and evaluate their evidence. Consider alternative explanations. Again, this is a difficult skill that doesn't come naturally to most people. Most of us are not used to thinking in a deliberate and rational manner when feeling anxious. However, this is the most important time to use this skill, because this is when you are most likely to think in biased ways! Let's apply this to an example. Sarah left the party early. Her thought was *They will probably notice it* (a form of emotional reasoning, because she used her feeling for the basis of her thinking). But let's consider some questions to help us formulate alternative possibilities:

- What might be another conclusion?

- What else might cause the event?

- What would a neutral observer think?

Perhaps people thought Sarah had to leave the party early because she had other things to do or didn't feel well physically or because she was tired, not because she was anxious. In fact, most people probably didn't even notice that she was gone. And those that did probably didn't think much of it. (The latter issue targets catastrophic thinking, which we will discuss shortly.)

Step 4: Clarify the outcome and determine the real probability. Now you can determine or calculate the *real probability*. Sarah noticed the thought: "If I mess things up, they will think I am incompetent and this will affect my son's education." This thought reflects both probability overestimation and catastrophic thinking. Using available information, you'll determine the actual likelihood of the predicted, negative outcome. To do this, you assess how many times a particular event has actually occurred, divided by the number of times the event could have occurred. What is the likelihood that Sarah's son's education is negatively affected if she messes up her speech? This is a more difficult calculation. What does it mean to "mess up" a presentation? What does it mean to be "incompetent"? How can this even impact her son's education? Putting aside the catastrophic and unclear nature of this concern, the probability that her son's education is in any way impacted by her presentation is virtually nonexistent. How and why would this be possible? The more specific we get, the more unlikely the outcome becomes. A crucially important tool to tackle thinking errors is to raise critical questions in order to increase specificity. Thinking errors tend to be driven by global and emotional concerns. Critical questions raise specificity and expose the irrationality of the thought.

Step 5: Contrast your initial (anxious) thought with alternative (non-anxious) interpretations. The final step is to directly compare alternative, more realistic thoughts (judgments, interpretations) with the initial thinking error. What do you make of the evidence, the alternative explanations, and the real probability? What is a more realistic possibility? A valuable guide for the level of rationality of a thought is its believability. You know that you are on the right track if the believability rating of a non-anxious interpretation is a lot higher than the believability rating of your initial anxious thought. You may simply rate each thought from 0 (not at all believable) to 100 (completely believable, absolutely true). If you don't rate the non-anxious thought as considerably more believable, you want to re-do steps 1 through 4. If an anxious thought remains high in believability considering all the evidence and other alternatives, it is probably not a thinking error but a very realistic fear or cause of concern.

If these five steps sound too complicated, just remember that you are (1) questioning your automatic thoughts and (2) considering possible alternatives.

The table below can help you go through this process. (You can find a blank copy of this table at http://www.newharbinger.com/51208.)

Sarah had to go through the steps a number of times until she reached the following conclusion:

Table 4: Contrasting Sarah's Anxious and Non-anxious Thoughts

	Thoughts	Believability (0–100)
After reviewing the evidence, rate the believability of the original thought.	Original Thought: I will mess up my speech (at the PTA meeting); they will think I am incompetent and this will affect my son's education.	20
What is a more realistic possibility? Rate the believability of this thought.	Alternative Thought: My performance will be fine. Most people won't even care. It won't impact my son's education.	80
What can I tell myself in the future?	There is nothing to worry about.	

It's not uncommon for people to *feel* like the alternative, non-anxious thoughts are not very believable. This is because of the nature of emotional reasoning. It's simply easier to *think* in anxious ways when you're *feeling* anxious, and it's difficult to think in alternative (or non-anxious) ways when we feel anxious. Going through these steps a number of times can activate and strengthen your healthy mind. Even small changes are major progress! With repeated practice and consideration of the alternatives, the believability of your anxious thoughts will continue to decrease.

In conclusion, probability overestimation involves making an inaccurate or unreasonable prediction that an unlikely event is highly probable. You can counter this by evaluating the evidence *for* and *against* the thought, exploring alternative explanations, and calculating the real probability. Remember that thoughts, rather than situations alone, drive our emotions and behaviors. Automatic thoughts are thoughts that occur quickly and often without conscious awareness. These thoughts can easily be biased, such as when we're making judgments about situations based on *feelings* rather than *facts*. Let's turn now to the other maladaptive thinking style: catastrophic thinking.

Catastrophic Thinking

This thinking error is often at the heart of SAD. People with social anxiety often exaggerate the negative consequences of an unpleasant social encounter. Catastrophic thinking actually includes two errors in thinking: (1) the incorrect belief that an uncomfortable social situation has negative, long-lasting, and irreversible consequences, and (2) the incorrect belief that there is little you can do to cope with it. Simply speaking, catastrophic thinking is responsible for your making a big deal out of something that is not.

True catastrophes are very rare. Dying is a real catastrophe. There is nothing you can do about that once you are dead. Then there are bad things that happen in life, such as losing a loved one, getting fired from your favorite job, experiencing a breakup or divorce, and so on. But even those situations are manageable, and you eventually find ways to cope with them. You learn to live without your loved one, you find another job, and you eventually get over the breakup or divorce. Things that seem horrible and unmanageable now are less distressing once you encounter them, in part because you find new ways to deal with them when you are confronted with them.

Being ridiculed, feeling embarrassed, or bombing out in a speech are certainly unpleasant experiences, but none of these is a catastrophe, no matter how bad they make you feel. You engage in catastrophic thinking if you adopt a thinking style that turns uncomfortable events into a crisis. In the case of social anxiety, this often happens where there are violations of social norms, perceived standards, and expectations.

Challenging Catastrophic Thinking

To challenge catastrophic thinking, you will first need to slow down your judgment by considering the *actual severity* of an outcome as well as what you'd realistically do to cope *if* the situation were to occur. One effective strategy to challenge catastrophic thinking is the "so what" approach. It involves thinking through the actual consequences of the feared outcome occurring in order to determine its actual severity and identify ways to cope. Here are the concrete steps to counter catastrophic thinking using the "so what" approach.

Step 1: Slow down and notice. To target catastrophic thinking, or any other maladaptive thinking error, you must first become aware that it's happening. As in the case of probability overestimation, catastrophic thinking happens quickly, usually in the form of an automatic thought, so you must slow down in order to catch it happening.

Step 2: Find words to describe your thoughts. This step involves putting words into thoughts. This means that you should try to formulate sentences starting with *I am thinking that...* You might even write down your thoughts on paper. This process can facilitate slowing down and increasing awareness.

Step 3: Give your thought a believability rating. Next, determine the believability of the thought. You obtain a believability rating by asking yourself, *How believable is this thought?* Rate the initial believability of the thought on a scale of 0 (not at all believable) to 100 (completely believable, absolutely true).

Step 4: Examine the consequences of the event. To examine the consequences of the event, you should now identify the true severity of the feared outcome. When people engage in catastrophic thinking, they exaggerate the severity. One effective way to realistically appraise the severity of the situation is to ask yourself: *So what?* As we discussed earlier, some things are, in fact, a really big deal, but most things are not. Losing your train of thought during a speech or spilling hot coffee over your colleague seems to be a very big deal in the moment. But the moment passes, and then another moment comes and other things seem to be a much bigger deal then. As a result, we slide seamlessly from one perceived catastrophe to the next. A powerful antidote to this tendency is to adopt a perspective that is illustrated on one of my favorite cartoons showing the Buddha with the text underneath saying "The root of all suffering is the giving of the fucks." To appreciate this, you don't need to be a nihilist or an apostle of the Big Lebowski's Dudeism, but it doesn't hurt either.

Obviously, we shouldn't confuse "so what?" with "who cares?." I am not suggesting that you shouldn't care about whether bad things happen or not. Rather, the goal is to develop a realistic perspective on the actual consequences. Think of the "so what" approach as a method of asking yourself questions like *So what happens next?* and *If that happens, then what?* This approach is about following the thought through to its logical outcome and then asking yourself, *So how bad would that be, really?*

Step 5: Identify your coping strategies. Even if an actual outcome matches your prediction and a catastrophe seems to happen, you have ways to cope with it. Your coping strategies are often much more effective than you first assumed. If you can cope with the outcome, it doesn't seem to be catastrophic after all. Spilling coffee over your colleague might not end up in a fist fight. Your coping strategies—apologizing and offering to pay the cleaning bill (which he will probably politely decline), then insisting on treating him to another coffee—will likely resolve the situation.

Identifying your coping strategies allows you to consider strategies that you could use if the negative outcome were to come true. We tend to forget the resources we have available to deal with a situation if it were to happen. You are less likely to think something is a big deal if you feel confident in your ability to handle it! To guide you in identifying your coping skills and strategies, there are several questions you can ask yourself:

- What am I afraid will happen?

- How could I deal with this?

- Has this bad event ever happened before?

- What did I do before?

- How did I handle it then?

It can be quite difficult to come up with coping strategies in the moment, especially when feeling anxious. To give you some hints, here are some examples of common coping strategies, resources, and personal characteristics that might remind you of effective approaches to use when the need arises. You'll notice that some of the items on this list will apply in some situations but not others. Read this list and circle any that you might use.

- Rely on the skills you have

- Wait to see what happens next

- Problem solve

- Ignore your mishap

- Find creative solutions

- Ask a friend for help

- Explain yourself

- Check the internet to get some ideas

- Apologize if you caused harm or damage

- Use self-deprecating humor to relax the situation

These are just some general ideas. The specific coping strategies you use in a given situation can look very different, of course. Some strategies can be useful in some situations, but they might be rather maladaptive in another context. For example, sometimes waiting, apologizing, or using humor can be the wrong approach. Context matters greatly. With time, you will develop a sense of which approach is adaptive and which is maladaptive in a given situation. There is no approach and no skill that is always right or always wrong.

Now that you've learned the steps of the "so what" approach, let's put it to practice with a recent example of a threatening situation in your own life. Take out a sheet of paper and make three columns. Label the second column "Thoughts" and the third column "Believability." (You can also find a blank copy of this table at http://www .newharbinger.com/51208.)

In the first row, briefly describe the threating situation in column one and the thoughts you had before and/or during this situation in column two. In the third column, rate how believable the thought is using a scale from 0 (not believable at all) to 100 (very believable). These responses represent the first three steps we just discussed: (1) slow down and notice, (2) find words to describe your thoughts, and (3) give your thought a believability rating. In the second row, record your thoughts about the consequences (step 4) and rate the believability of these thoughts. In the third row, write down your thoughts of what coping strategies you can use (step 5) and rate their believability—in other words, how likely you will be to use them. Finally, in the last row, write down an adaptive thought about the threatening situation—one that would help to alleviate your anxiety—and its believability rating.

Let's look at how Sarah completed this table. Imagine her speech during the PTA meeting was, in fact, quite bad. She got up, stammered something unintelligible, and sat back down again. She was afraid this would happen. What a catastrophe. Or was it?

Table 5: Sarah's Catastrophic Thought

	Thoughts	Believability
Catastrophic Thought	Everybody thinks I am incompetent.	100
Consequences (So What?)	Some people might think I am incompetent but I don't care. Others might not have noticed or didn't care.	20
Coping Strategies	I will speak up again next time. If I feel I am getting tongue-tied again, I might make a joke about myself.	30
Adaptive Thought	Messing up a speech is no big deal.	20

Notice that after she messed up her speech, Sarah first rated her thought "Everybody thinks I am incompetent" as highly believable (100 on a 0–100-point scale) and rated her adaptive thought (*Messing up a speech is no big deal*) as very low in believability. The more often she engages in this exercise, the more the believability of her adaptive thoughts will increase and the more her maladaptive thoughts will decrease. It takes time. But it will happen in time by trying out different coping strategies.

Thinking Errors in Daily Life

Very often an anxious thought is due to both probability overestimation and catastrophic thinking. This is because we often believe that a negative outcome is much more likely than it actually is, and we also assume the outcome would result in disaster if it did come true. As a result, these thinking errors can amplify each other. This was the case with Sarah's thought around her speech during the PTA meeting. She thought she would certainly mess up her speech (a probability overestimation) and that others would judge her negatively for it, even impacting her son's education (a catastrophic thought).

It can be helpful to separate the thought into these two maladaptive thinking styles and use the techniques described above for each individual part. Separating thinking errors into catastrophic thinking and probability overestimation helps break the amplifying cycle. Again, you target probability overestimation by examining the evidence for and against such beliefs. Sometimes (such as in the case of the plane crash example), you can even calculate the odds that these things will happen, and you will see that the probability of it occurring may not be as high as you initially thought. You target catastrophic thinking with the "so what" approach. It's typically a chain of thoughts and consequences and at the end, you might just end up with a thought "people will think badly of me" or "I will be embarrassed" or "people will judge me negatively." Sure, that's not a pleasant thing. But so what? It's certainly not a catastrophe.

What if you can't tell the difference between probability overestimation and catastrophizing? That's okay. It's more important that you learn to slow down and notice and challenge your thinking than it is to correctly categorize each thought. See what works for you to most effectively challenge your thinking errors and find a more realistic or alternative viewpoint. Don't remain a prisoner of your own mind.

But going through those steps in your mind will only get you so far. The crucial piece that will likely change your life is to implement these strategies by generating real challenges for yourself. This could mean confronting yourself with rather uncomfortable social situations in order to examine their real threat by challenging your thinking errors. This is what I call *social mishap exposures*, and you will learn how to do this in the chapters that follow. I don't want to give you too much more information so as not to scare you too much; just enough to pique your interest. Ready? Here we go.

CHAPTER 5

Confronting Social Mishaps

The previous chapters gave you a number of very useful tools already. Putting them together creates a powerful approach to deal with social anxiety: social mishap exposures. Remember that exposure procedures are highly effective. Exposure here means that you are confronting the feared social situation while eliminating any type of avoidance strategies and safety behaviors and experiencing that anxiety goes down all by itself. Also remember that thinking errors make you believe that an unpleasant event during a social situation is very likely to happen and that this event would have negative, long-lasting, and irreversible consequences.

A highly effective strategy to fight all of these issues is using exposure practices as real-life experiments to examine the validity of your beliefs. For example, if you are worried about appearing crazy, you can probably come up with a long list of things you definitely don't want to do in public, such as talking to nonliving things. How do you think museum goers would respond if you had an intimate discussion with a bronze statue? Some would probably think you're crazy. What would that mean? What would happen next? Would they throw you out of the museum? Or would somebody call the police or the ambulance to get you committed to a psychiatric ward and lock you up for years? Or perhaps they would just laugh? Would others even notice? The only way to find out is to do it!

Consider the following famous and classic experiment by Richard Solomon and Lyman Wynne (1953). The researchers put a dog into a box with two compartments separated by a small wall. The dog was able to jump

over the wall from one compartment to the other. One of the compartments had a food tray, encouraging the dog to spend most of the time in
that half. The same compartment also had a light, and the floor of this
compartment contained wires that sent a painful (but not dangerous) electric shock to the dog (sorry, dog lovers and owners—I am one myself). For
a few trials, the researchers administered the shock right after the light was
turned on. In other words, for the dog, the light signaled the upcoming
administration of the shock. The dog quickly learned to avoid the shock by
jumping over to the other compartment as soon as the light went off. But
what happened when the shock was no longer administered? The light still
went on, but no shock followed. You probably guessed right—the dog kept
jumping over to the other compartment even though the light no longer
signaled shock. The only way for the dog to learn that the light no longer
signals shock is to stay in the compartment to see what actually happens.

What does this have to do with your social anxiety? You avoid social
encounters (or use safety behaviors) when you feel threatened. Many events
in your life might have contributed to it. Perhaps you learned from your
parents to be careful in social situations. Perhaps you are just a shy and careful
person. But the reasons that contributed to it from your past (the initiating
factors) are not that important in order to change the problem. What's
important are the reasons you keep avoiding (the maintaining factors). You
do this because you expect that something bad might happen (even though
you are wrong), and those avoidance strategies are intended to prevent this
fictitious danger from happening. But as long as you keep using avoidance
strategies, you will never know whether the situation is, in fact, dangerous.
The only way to find out is to see what actually happens without using them!

Exposures to social situations are considerably more complex (but more
humane) than the experiment by Solomon and Wynne. But still, the basic
idea remains: you will need to expose yourself to those dreaded situations
and experience what happens. Translated to social anxiety, if you keep
avoiding parties because you expect something horrible will happen to you
(whatever that might be), you will never find out that nothing horrible will
happen to you at those parties. You never know unless you try. Just as the
dog keeps avoiding a perfectly safe place, you keep avoiding the same
because of your inaccurate assumptions. As long as both of you avoid,

anxiety will persist. Exposure is the only way to put your anxious predictions to the test in order to refute them and correct your misconceptions. This is the only way to free yourself from the shackles of SAD. Exposure will allow you to compare the actual outcome with the anticipated outcome. If there's a mismatch, it's time to adopt a more realistic view. And there is a mismatch if the bad outcome is a lot less likely to happen than anticipated, and even if it did happen, you finds ways to cope with it. In essence, social mishap exposure will give you an opportunity to find out that it is not nearly as bad as you think it is, and there are ways to cope with it. And this has dramatic implications. These practices, when done right, touch on virtually every single maintaining factor we discussed earlier. But let's go one step at a time.

Prepare for the Exposure

The first step in creating an exposure practice is to prepare for it. We'll use Sarah's example to illustrate. For this preparation, we need to understand why Sarah perceives a situation as threatening and what Sarah has been doing to deal with it. To discover which maintaining factors are most relevant for Sarah, we administered the "Approach to Social Situations Scale" from chapter 2.

Sarah's Approach to Social Situations
(Copyright Stefan G. Hofmann, 2022)

1. I believe that the expectations of me in social situations are very high.

    0—1—2—3—4—5—6—7—8—**9**—10

2. I am often not quite clear about what I personally want to achieve in a social situation.

    0—1—2—3—4—5—6—7—8—**9**—10

3. I tend to focus my attention toward myself when I am in a social situation.

    0—1—2—3—4—5—6—7—8—**9**—10

4. I tend to overestimate how bad a social situation can turn out.

    0—1—2—3—4—5—6—**7**—8—9—10

5. I believe that my social skills to handle social situations are poor.

    0—1—2—3—4—5—6—**7**—8—9—10

6. I don't like myself very much when it comes to social situations.

    0—1—2—3—4—5—6—7—8—**9**—10

7. I have little control over my anxiety in social situations.

    0—1—2—3—4—5—6—7—**8**—9—10

8. I think that people can tell when I am anxious in social situations.

    0—1—2—3—4—5—6—7—**8**—9—10

9. I usually expect that something bad will happen to me in a social situation.

    0—1—2—3—4—5—6—**7**—8—9—10

10. I tend to dwell on social situations after they happen.

    0—1—2—3—4—**5**—6—7—8—9—10

11. I often avoid social situations.

    0—1—2—**3**—4—5—6—7—8—9—10

12. I often do things that make me feel less uncomfortable when I am in social situations.

    0—1—2—**3**—4—5—6—7—8—9—10

We learn that Sarah rated many items quite high, except her avoidance safety behaviors. She did not think she often avoids or does anything to make herself feel less uncomfortable in social situations. This is not to say that self-report is generally unreliable. It simply means that avoidance behaviors are often difficult to catch. Oftentimes my clients do not think that they avoid or use any safety behaviors. Remember that these behaviors can be quite subtle. Plus, after years of living with SAD, people have built their lives around SAD and avoidance becomes second nature. My point here is that avoidance always plays an important role, even if people don't realize it. Let's drill into the details of a particular situation.

Remember figure 2 (chapter 2) summarizing the various maintaining factors of SAD? Let's use Sarah's example of when she had to speak at the PTA meeting. Based on what we know, we can identify the following maintaining factors (some of the information has been elicited in detailed follow-up conversations).

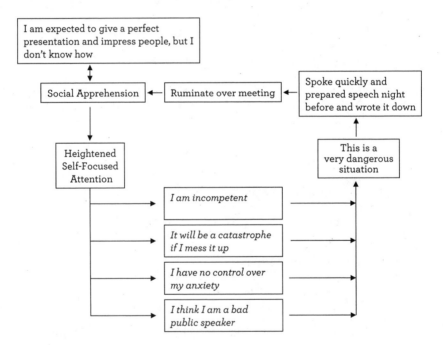

Figure 7: Reasons Sarah Is Afraid to Give Presentation During PTA Meeting (copyright Stefan G. Hofmann, 2022)

Sarah is showing a few of the thinking errors we discussed (*I am incompetent, it will be a catastrophe if I mess it up*). To deal with her anxiety, she prepared the presentation the night before and even wrote it down. This is a rather unusual thing for a parent to do when they speak at their PTA meeting. Sarah did this as a way to deal with her social anxiety. She also rehearsed it, spoke quickly, and avoided eye contact. All of these strategies count as avoidance strategies based on our definition earlier (*anything you do or don't do that keeps you from facing your fear*). Just like the dog in Solomon and Wynne's experiment, Sarah does not give herself a chance to examine whether the situation is, in fact, dangerous.

We notice a number of other factors responsible for Sarah's anxiety. Her social anxiety comes from her perception that the PTA has high standards and the fact that she isn't sure what makes one accepted by the group. She believes she is expected to give a perfect presentation and even needs to impress people. But this goal is as unrealistic as it is unspecific and unclear. Other parents at the meetings, in contrast, have very clear and realistic goals. One parent wanted teachers to assign less homework for their children. Another wanted tutoring services for her child. Neither of them seemed to care what others think of them. Sarah's presentation was not overly task-focused. She thanked the teachers and staff for creating a good environment for her son, but also mentioned the dirty toilets. She didn't really have a specific goal in mind. She just wanted people to know and like her. Her social standards were high and her goals poorly defined.

Sarah's anxiety shot up as soon as she started speaking. She focused her attention inwardly, toward herself, leaving little attention for her speech content and delivery. She felt incompetent, felt that she had no control over her anxiety, and was convinced that she is simply a bad speaker. As mentioned above, in addition to overpreparing, she also spoke quickly to rush through her presentation.

One important feature of Sarah's exposure assignment is to eliminate her avoidance strategies. This means that (1) she cannot prepare her presentation and write it down, and (2) she will have to speak slowly. But to make this exposure most successful, we might want to target other maintaining factors as well.

Most important for the social mishap exposure are her perceived standards and goals and her estimation of social cost. Sarah believes that she is expected to give a perfect presentation and impress people, but she doesn't really know how (i.e., she shows high perceived social standards and has poorly defined goals). Also, she believes that it would be a catastrophe if she messes things up (high estimated social cost). It follows that the most effective exposure for Sarah is to give an unprepared presentation with a very specific goal (e.g., better school lunches) delivered very slowly and with some prepared stutters and stammers (which is why I call this "social mishap exposure"). Sarah will then need to (1) predict what will happen (e.g., will people cut her off or laugh at her?) and (2) compare what she predicted to what actually did happen.

The general rules are:

1.   Identify what exactly makes the situation so anxiety provoking.

2.   Identify and eliminate any safety behaviors and other avoidance strategies.

3.   Determine the main goal you want to achieve. Be specific.

4.   Specify what kind of social mishaps you are afraid of, and what the social consequences would be.

What are the most fear-provoking aspects of a social situation to you? Please select a specific fear-provoking social situation and write down your answers to the questions below. (This worksheet is also available at http://www.newharbinger.com/51208.) Then see if you can construct a figure similar to figure 7. Try to complete the sentence with one or a few examples (add more if needed).

Social Situation Fear Analysis

The social situation is uncomfortable because:

1.

2.

Your response gets to social apprehension.

I believe that other people expect me to be:

1.

2.

This gets to social standards.

If I am confronted with this social situation, I am most concerned/worried that:

1.

2.

3.

4.

Take your time thinking about this one. Is it because your skills are inadequate and you are unable to perform? Or are you concerned that your anxiety is out of control? Or that you will be rejected?

In order to bring down my anxiety, I tend to do the following:

1.

2.

3.

This obviously gets to the various avoidance strategies that keep your anxiety alive. Make sure you eliminate all of them as you expose yourself to your social fears.

Some people find it helpful to imagine the scenario as vividly as possible. You might even write down this image so you can compare your image of what would happen to what actually did happen. You will be surprised.

Implement the Exposure

Now it's time to test out your predictions. Remember, social situations often appear fear provoking because you believe that social mishaps are likely and costly. An effective strategy to test it out is to engage in real social mishap exposure. In other words, let's really mess up the social situation and see what actually happens! There is no need to do anything that gets you into real trouble (e.g., gets you fired, thrown in jail, or divorced—unless any of those are desirable outcomes for you). Instead, choose situations that are within socially acceptable norms for most people and do not violate legal boundaries or harm others. Doing this might be one of the most frightening things you could ever imagine, but it becomes surprisingly easy with time. For many, these exposures are highly effective because they simultaneously target some of the core problems in a powerful way. Many people find them incredibly liberating. Try it out. See what happens.

A few years ago, Jessica Pan, a writer for *The Guardian* and book author, called me from London to discuss her specific case of social anxiety. After a long conversation, she asked me to give her specific instructions to deal with her fear of appearing stupid in public. I suggested that she voluntarily and willingly create a situation where she would see how people respond if she does something very stupid. Specifically, I suggested she approach five random people in the tube (the London subway) and ask each of them the following question: "Excuse me, do you know if England has a queen and if so, what is her name?" (This was before Queen Elizabeth had passed.) She expected that some people would laugh at her and others would be rude and angry. She did it. But nobody was rude. Nobody laughed at her. Instead, most people simply answered the question. Interestingly, two of them thought that the name of the reigning queen was Victoria. She wrote about this experience in detail in her book *Sorry I'm Late, I Didn't Want to Come* (Pan 2019). Some examples I've used with my clients in the past include:

- Stand right in front of Fenway Park (Boston's Red Sox baseball stadium) and ask ten people, over a period of one hour, "Excuse me, how do I get to Fenway Park?"

- Go into Starbucks, order a croissant, drop it on the floor, and tell the cashier, "I just dropped my croissant on the floor and would like to get a new one, but I don't want to pay for it."

- Go to a fancy bar, order a glass of tap water, and ask the bartender if they have seen the movie *When Harry Met Sally* and, if so, who the actors were.

- Stand in front of a subway station and sing "Mary Had a Little Lamb" three times in a row.

- Engage in a "discussion" with a bronze statue in a museum for five minutes.

Figure 8: How Will Other People Respond if You Talk to a Bronze Statue in a Museum? (copyright Stefan G. Hofmann)

- Go to a drug store, ask for some condoms, and when the pharmacist brings them, ask, "Is this the smallest size you have?" Regardless of the answer, simply leave without a word.

- Go to every man sitting at a table in a crowded restaurant and ask, "Are you Barack Obama?"

- Go to a bookstore and say to a clerk, "Hi, I am looking for a book on farting." Side note: There are actually such books. I know because I practiced it myself. Both are children's books by the title, *Everybody Poops*, and *The Gas We Pass*.

Let's zoom into some of these examples. One of Sarah's catastrophic thoughts is "It will be a catastrophe if I mess up a speech." This means that Sarah should create a situation to experience what would actually happen if she did mess up her speech. There are many ways she could do it, and it would be a good idea for her to try out a few to see what works best. For example, she might just stop abruptly and say, "I forgot what I wanted to say."

Let's look at another person with other types of social fears. Remember Carrie, the fifty-year-old postal worker? Here is a dialogue between Carrie and their therapist leading up to this social mishap exposure:

Therapist: So, Sarah, let's try to test out some of the concerns you have in social situations. You had mentioned that one of your concerns is that you appear crazy to others. I know that you enjoy singing. Is there a way to test out your prediction? What would make you look crazy when you sing in front of other people?

Carrie: Well, I could stand on the sidewalk and sing something silly.

Therapist: Great idea! Like what? A children's song? Maybe "Mary Had a Little Lamb"?

Carrie: Yes, people would definitely think I'm crazy if I stand on the sidewalk and sing "Mary Had a Little Lamb."

Therapist: That's great. Is this enough to make you look crazy? Is there anything else you could do in addition?

Carrie: I'm not sure. But this would definitely be something that would make me look crazy.

Therapist: Great. Let's do it. Let's go outside. I would like you to stand in front of the subway station and loudly sing "Mary Had a Little Lamb" three times in a row.

Carrie: Wow. Okay. That is freaking me out.

Therapist: What is your anxiety on a 0–100-point scale?

Carrie: Right now it's maybe 70, but I'm sure it will be 100 when we go out there. Will you be there with me?

Therapist: I will be half a block away so I can hear and see you and others. I don't want to be a safety person for you. What do you think other people will do? What are your predictions?

Carrie: Well, I think people will stand around me and laugh at me and somebody will probably call the cops to get me off the street.

Therapist: Great. Thanks. So you expect that people will gather around you and make fun of you and the police will come as well. What is your prediction that people will gather around you, that they will make fun of you, and the police will come, on a 0–100-point scale?

Carrie: I don't know. Maybe 90?

Therapist: Great. We had discussed a particular thinking error called probability overestimation, which is overestimating the likelihood of a bad event that is not likely to occur. Do you think that 90 is correct?

Carrie: I don't know. Probably not. But this is what it feels like.

Therapist: I understand. There is another thinking error called emotional reasoning, which means that you're thinking in an anxious way because you feel anxious. But this thought might not match reality. The best way to get clarity and to correct these thinking errors is to test your beliefs. What do you think?

Carrie: Okay, I will try.

Although Carrie thought that their anxiety would be at 100, they were surprised that their anxiety went down pretty quickly in the first few minutes. To their surprise, nothing really happened. People simply walked by, and most didn't even acknowledge Carrie's presence; a few people smiled. No crowd gathered around them; nobody made fun of them; no police came. In the end Carrie realized that it wasn't nearly as bad as they thought it would be. Carrie had to acknowledge that she needed to correct the probability she had assigned to the feared scenario that people would be standing around them and making fun of them. But what if this actually did happen? Let's listen in to more of the dialogue between Carrie and their therapist.

Therapist: So let's assume the worst thing will, in fact, happen. Can you summarize for me again what that would be?

Carrie: I don't know. Maybe a group of people will gather and they will make fun of me or will call the police.

Therapist: Okay. These are two predictions. Let's test one at a time. Let's focus on the former. So let's assume a group of five or so people would gather around you, pointing their fingers at you and making fun of you. Would they be cursing you? Shouting at you?

Carrie: I'm not sure. Maybe they will giggle and point their fingers at me?

Therapist: Because they are judging you negatively?

Carrie: Yes.

Therapist: Have you been judged negatively in the past?

Carrie: Of course, many times.

Therapist: Of course, we all have had this experience. It feels very bad. But we survive and life goes on. You obviously also survived this situation, because you are sitting here telling me about it. My point is that being judged negatively is quite common. It's an unpleasant but short-lasting experience. We have ways to cope with it. You have ways to cope with it. We call this thinking error *catastrophic thinking*. It means that we are making a big deal out of something that is not. Real catastrophes do exist, such as death. But being judged negatively by another person is not a catastrophe.

Carrie's exposure exercises should be tailored to their specific concerns. For example, they might modify their singing exposure by wearing a crazy looking hat to appear even crazier, or by singing a song off key to be judged even more negatively.

Let's see what kind of exercises target your specific concern. Write down a dialogue between your *courageous self* and your *anxious self*. Your courageous self takes on the role of the therapist, whereas your anxious self may sound just like Carrie and Sarah.

Your courageous self might prompt your anxious self with questions such as *What are you most worried about? Are you worried about being judged negatively? Appearing crazy? Appearing rude? Appearing stupid?* Go ahead and do this on a sheet of paper with the goal of generating very specific exposure exercises for your anxious self to test out your predictions. Once you have designed your social mishap exposure exercises(s), try them out and see what happens.

These exercises are most effective if they are tailored to your idiosyncratic fears and concerns. What happens as a result of these exercises is that you gain another perspective that changes the way you feel. This is because the way you *think* and how you perceive a situation has an enormous influence on the way you *feel*. This means that *you have control over the way you feel by changing the way you think.*

Beliefs are our general views of what's right and what's wrong; what's good and what's bad; what's desirable and what's undesirable. They are the basic assumptions about how the world, the future, and we ourselves ought to behave. Some of these beliefs can also be anxious beliefs. Anxious beliefs are often hard to question and dispute because they are typically taken for fact. They feel like part of us, part of our personality. They are the "shoulds" and "shouldn'ts." Many of these beliefs are desirable and help us function in this world. "You should avoid harming other people," "You should be honest," "You should not exploit other people," and so on. These are examples of very adaptive and valuable beliefs. Other beliefs, on the other hand, are irrational, maladaptive, and dysfunctional. They restrict us, inhibit us, and make us prisoners of our own convictions. Many irrational beliefs have to do with perfectionism. "You should not show anxiety or weakness in front of other people," "You shouldn't make any mistakes when performing in social situations," or "Every audience member should love your speech." Guess what—nobody is perfect. Not even you.

Is it really such a big deal if you stumble over a word, loose your train of thought for a few seconds, or blush in front of people? Most people might not even notice it. And even if they do, they probably won't mind that much. In fact, people who make little mistakes are typically perceived as more likeable than those who don't make any mistakes. Being imperfect is human. Of course, you know this already in principle. And it is probably easy to give this advice to a good friend or your child. However, if you are like most people with social anxiety, you are much less forgiving and compassionate toward yourself. Your self-critical part is simply too dominant. In a way, you need to relearn to accept yourself the way you are. This will be the main focus of the next chapter.

Compare and Review the Exposure

After completing a social mishap exposure, it is important to reflect back and compare what you expected would happen to what actually did happen.

This generates a discrepancy between expected and actual, leading to a radical shift in your perception. After therapy for SAD, people often summarize their lessons learned as follows:

1. The more you think other people expect from you, the greater your anxiety. These expectations may not be correct.

2. It is important to clearly define the goals of a social situation. Otherwise, we don't know whether or not we have reached them and whether or not it has been a success.

3. The more you focus on yourself in a social situation, the more anxious you feel.

4. People cannot feel anxious if they feel comfortable the way they are in social situations.

5. Social mishaps are normal; it is no big deal if they do happen.

6. Other people can't see how anxious you are, and you're more in control of your anxiety than you think you are.

7. Your social skills are most likely better than you think they are. If not, then adjust your standards.

8. Safety behaviors and other forms of avoidance lead to the maintenance and worsening of anxiety.

We will touch on some of these lessons again in later chapters.

To conclude, social anxiety is not really the primary problem. The problem is your way of thinking about yourself and social situations and your response to them. As you change your approach, you will see a dramatic change in your anxiety as a result. But this will take some time and require patience on your part. Your new approach to social situations is like a new exercise routine you learned in a gym. It requires using muscles you didn't even know you had. It's very uncomfortable at the beginning. But the more you do it, the easier it gets and the closer you get to your desired goals—to live the life you want to live!

CHAPTER 6

Accepting Yourself

Accepting yourself and the conditions around you is the most effective strategy for dealing with the things about social situations, and even your emotional response to them, that can't be changed easily. Rather than fighting and being frustrated with a situation or yourself, you might want to pursue a different approach: Accept things, including yourself.

How do you feel about yourself when you are around others? Many people with social anxiety don't like themselves as a social object. Perhaps you can relate to this? Do you feel uncomfortable when looking at a picture of yourself? Does your smile look fake to you? Are your teeth too big? Do you notice your awkward moves in a video clip of yourself? Do you dislike the tone and pitch of your voice? This is not at all unusual for people with social anxiety. But why do socially anxious people dislike looking at themselves, even if there is no one else around who could possibly evaluate them negatively? Well, in fact there is a person evaluating you negatively. You yourself!

Social anxiety has a lot to do with negative self-perception. If you don't accept yourself for the way you are, you will naturally assume that nobody else would accept you for the way you are. Your belief of what other people think of you is thus in part a reflection of what you think of yourself. Therefore, changing the way you perceive yourself will change your belief of what other people think of you. This, in turn, determines your level of discomfort and anxiety in a social situation. Let's drill down into self-perception, what it is, and how to change it. It might just hit the core of your social anxiety.

Social Anxiety and the Self

There are three types of belief systems: thoughts about the self, thoughts about the world, and thoughts about the future. These three belief systems have been termed the "cognitive triad" (Beck and Emery 1985). Here we will focus on thoughts about the self. Some of these thoughts are positive, others are negative. For example, *I am open minded* is a positive self-focused thought, whereas *I am impatient* is a negative self-focused thought. Some of these self-focused thoughts are also social in nature. For example, *I am trustworthy* is a positive self-focused thought, whereas *I am socially incompetent* is a negative self-focused thought. I'm sure you can think of many more examples. Please write them down, without thinking too much about them. Who are you? How would you describe yourself? These thoughts define you as a social being—as an object in our own social world.

We know that effective treatments for SAD lead to changes in the way we think and the way we perceive our social environment and ourselves as social objects. This not only includes the perception of danger in social situations, but also the perception of our social skills to master the situation and the perception of control over our anxiety response in social situations.

Such changes are not unique to the treatment of SAD. In fact, social anxiety shares many similarities with other types of anxiety. But social anxiety differs from other forms of anxiety because it concerns your evaluation and perception of yourself. Unlike people who are anxious about dogs, for example, a person anxious about giving a speech is not so much concerned about physical harm, but much more about the potential harm to the self. Many socially anxious people tend to be very concerned about how they come across to others and, as a result, are very sensitive to others' evaluations of them. They are constantly monitoring themselves in social situations and are overly critical toward themselves.

Social psychologists refer to this phenomenon as "public self-consciousness" (because it refers to the public aspects of the self). Public self-consciousness leads to self-awareness, which is a common aspect of social anxiety. Social anxiety can create a feedback loop wherein excessive self-consciousness makes you act as awkward as you feel, which reinforces the mistaken idea that you need to closely monitor your social performance.

Attention is of only limited capacity. If a lot of your attention is occupied by one task (such as self-monitoring processes), less attention is available for other things (such as task performance). That's why most people find it difficult to follow two dinner conversations at the same time.

Self-focused attention, depression, social performance, and social anxiety are therefore closely connected. The critical piece that leads to the *maintenance* of social anxiety is self-focused attention: greater social anxiety leads to greater self-focused attention in the social situation. In other words, the more time you spend thinking about how you come across in social situations, the more social anxiety you will feel. The attention that could be used for successful social performance (e.g., speech, talking, telling a story, attentively listening to somebody) is then used for monitoring yourself. You might engage in something called self-management—trying to control your performance and how you look. Not surprisingly, this generates even more anxiety, establishing a vicious cycle (figure 9).

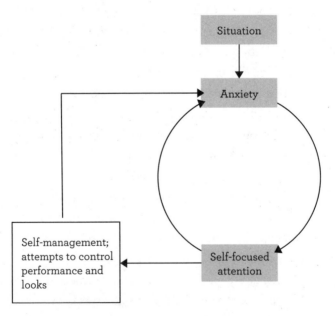

Figure 9: The Role of Self-Focused Attention in Social Anxiety (copyright Stefan G. Hofmann, 2022)

Effective psychological treatment of social anxiety leads to decreased self-focused attention. In fact, a change in self-focused attention is directly related to therapeutic gains, as we have shown in our studies (Hofmann 2000; Hofmann et al. 2004). In one study (Hofmann 2000), we treated patients with SAD using CBT. Before and after treatment, we assessed participants' level of social anxiety and asked them to perform a social test. This test consisted of four real social tasks (making a speech in front of one male and one female person, initiating and maintaining a conversation with a stranger, expressing disagreement to a stranger, and solving simple mathematical problems on a chalkboard while two people were watching them). Each task lasted for ten minutes and was preceded by a three-minute anticipation period. At the end of the three-minute anticipation period, participants were asked to write down any thoughts they had during this three-minute anticipation period.

Participants reported a total of 506 thoughts. Two raters classified each thought into one of nine mutually exclusive categories (listed here with examples): (1) positive task-focused thoughts ("this will be an easy task"); (2) negative task-focused thoughts ("these are difficult tests"); (3) neutral task-focused thoughts ("I was thinking about what I would talk about"); (4) positive self-focused thoughts ("I can handle this"); (5) negative self-focused thoughts ("I am worried about making a fool of myself"); (6) neutral self-focused thoughts ("I'm tired"); (7) positive other-focused thoughts ("I am enjoying the view out the window"); (8) negative other-focused thoughts ("I'm worrying about doing taxes over the weekend"); and (9) neutral other-focused thoughts (e.g., "I was thinking about the pros and cons of living in Boston versus living somewhere else").

The results showed that only changes in negative self-focused thoughts were highly correlated with treatment-induced changes in social anxiety. In other words, the more people improved in their social anxiety during treatment, the fewer negative self-focused thoughts they reported before these social tasks. In a larger follow-up study, we again found that psychological treatment was specifically associated with a significant reduction in the frequency of negative self-focused thoughts (Hofmann et al. 2004). These results suggest that SAD is a disorder of self-perception in that people with

SAD view themselves very negatively as a social object. For treatment to be effective, the intervention needs to reduce negative self-perception.

Being recorded on a video camera and looking in a mirror both enhance self-awareness, leaving fewer attentional resources for optimal task performance. In a way, many people with social anxiety feel constantly under observation by others, as if a camera were recording them all the time. Research shows, however, that there is no obvious difference in social skills between mildly and highly socially anxious (and self-conscious) people under low self-focused conditions (i.e., when there is no video camera or mirror present). The negative impact of self-focused attention on social performance is very subtle and barely visible to the untrained eye. But still, the constant self-monitoring can be exhausting and bring down your mood. In contrast, being in a good mood is often associated with less self-focused attention and also less social anxiety. This means that reducing self-focused attention—particularly negative self-focused attention—will not only lower your social anxiety, it will also improve your mood. Once you feel comfortable with the way you are, you will have less of a need to self-monitor and social anxiety will vanish.

Exposure to Mirror Image and Own Voice

Remember our discussion about eye contact earlier in the book? It appears that people with SAD show an exaggerated response to human faces and especially direct eye contact. Looking directly at yourself in the mirror can be quite effective in decreasing your exaggerated response to faces and eyes. Exposure to your own mirror image increases self-focused attention. You will have the urge to check yourself, your looks, and your appearance. Resist this urge. Go into your bathroom, lock the door, and look at yourself in the mirror for ten minutes. Do nothing else. Just look at yourself without judgment. Don't try to look good and don't check yourself. Instead, simply look at your face and your eyes as if they belong to another person you would like to meet. Experience your own presence. As you do this, you expose yourself to your own self—not your external appearance. If it's uncomfortable, you are onto something. Do this every day. Keep going until it gets easier. If it doesn't do anything for you, move on.

People with SAD also often dislike hearing their own voice. But your voice is part of your own self. Don't try to change it. Accept it as it is. Similar to the mirror exposure exercise, record your own voice. Ideally, record a speech on your smartphone about a subject you don't know much about. The more imperfect the speech, the better. Listen to this recording over and over again. At the beginning it will feel awkward and strange. You will notice the many pauses and mistakes you made. That's good. Just listen to it. You might even want to combine it with the mirror exposure. The goal is to accept yourself the way you are—with all your imperfections and awkward looks and appearances. Over time, the discomfort will eventually lessen. This is a normal process, which is called *habituation*. All you need to do is expose yourself without trying to make it easier for yourself. It will get easier by itself with time.

Self-Focused Attention Training

In order to perceive aspects of your own self, you need to direct attention toward yourself. But attention is of limited capacity. If you focus your attention on yourself, less attention is available for your actual social performance as well as anything else, such as enjoying the moment and making meaningful connections with people. This, of course, then further increases your anxiety.

You can focus your attention on different things during a social performance task. For example, you may focus on your bodily sensations (*My heart is racing, I wonder if they can see me sweat*), your appearance (*I should not have worn this dress, I hope they don't notice my pimple*), or your behaviors (*I am moving around too much, Why am I stuttering so much?*). In each case, your attention is being drawn away from your task performance and directed toward yourself.

It is normal to have some of these thoughts sometimes. But it is a problem if you have a lot of these thoughts most of the time. If they arise, let them come and let them go. Gently refocus your thoughts on your task and move on. In order to do this, you need to practice shifting your attention away from yourself. You can do this by simply directing the focus to where you want it to go. This requires some flexibility, which can be trained. Here is an example of such a simple training I did with Sarah:

Right before Sarah is about to speak, I manipulated her attentional focus by asking her to

1. focus on and describe her anxiety symptoms and self (30 seconds),

2. focus on and describe the environment (30 seconds), and

3. focus on and summarize her speech (30 seconds).

Here is how this played out:

Therapist: What is your anxiety right now on a scale from 0 (no anxiety) to 10 (extreme anxiety)?

Sarah: It is high…maybe an 8?

Therapist: What does an anxiety of 8 feel like? Please move your attention inward and tell me what is going on in your body.

Sarah: I feel like my heart is racing, my palms are sweating, and my mouth is dry.

Therapist: Thanks. What else do you notice inside yourself? What kind of thoughts are going through your mind?

Sarah: I am about to make a fool of myself because I don't really know much about the topic.

Therapist: Okay. What is your anxiety now on a scale from 0–10?

Sarah: It has not changed. Maybe it even went down a little. Maybe a 7?

Therapist: Okay. Now please look around. What are the things in the environment that make you anxious?

Sarah: You are sitting here, looking at me in anticipation. This makes me feel very uncomfortable.

Therapist: Great. And what is your anxiety now?

Sarah: The same: about an 7 or 8.

Therapist: Now please tell me what else you see in the environment that does not increase your anxiety.

Sarah: I see a picture on each wall. I see the plant.

Therapist: Anything else?

Sarah: The carpet. And I see the papers on the desk in the back and the books on the shelves. The lamp looks nice.

Therapist: Great work! What is your anxiety at this very moment on a scale from 0 to 10?

Sarah: Not much different. But maybe a little bit down because I was distracting myself. Maybe a 7 and a half.

Therapist: Thanks. Now please focus on your talk you are about to give. Focus on the topic at hand and give me a one- to two-sentence summary of your talk.

Sarah: I want to tell people about global warming.

Therapist: Excellent. What is your anxiety now?

Sarah: It just went up. 8.

Therapist: Thanks. Please tell me what goals you would like to meet. Without referring to your anxiety, what would make this situation a success? Are there any behaviors or other things you could do that would make the situation a success?

Sarah: Just being able to speak for three minutes would be a success.

Therapist: I agree. What else? Are there any behaviors—gestures, eye contact, et cetera, that would make it a success?

Sarah: I guess having eye contact with people.

Therapist: Great. So the goal is to speak for three minutes and to make eye contact with at least three people?

Sarah: Okay.

Therapist: Ready to start?

Sarah: Yes.

Notice that I asked Sarah about her anxiety after each attentional shift. This was because I wanted to examine a link between directing her attention to fear-relevant and fear-irrelevant cues and changes in her subjective anxiety. Even if this link cannot be easily demonstrated, this exercise demonstrates that attentional focus is under voluntary control and contributes to anxiety.

Enhancing Positive Feelings Toward Self and Others

Many people with social anxiety are overly critical of themselves (which often makes them very perfectionistic) and frequently monitor themselves in order to find all the negative aspects they don't like. Moreover, they assume that other people also see those flaws. The negative view of the self is probably the reason why social anxiety is so closely associated with depression in many people. Let's take Carrie from chapter 1 as an example. Carrie shows a very negative view of themself. They live a very isolated life but desire social contact. One reason for their social anxiety is negative self-perception and self-criticism.

Reducing self-criticism (which goes along with self-acceptance) builds self-confidence. Instead of trying to improve your social skills and the way you come across to other people, you may simply accept your weaknesses, enjoy your strengths, and be content with the way you are. Don't be perfect, show some weaknesses in front of other people, just be yourself. This is easier said than done. Changing your self-perception takes some time, but it can be accomplished. One powerful practice to do this is called *loving-kindness* (or *metta*) *meditation*.

The word "love" can have different meanings. Love can be romantic between two partners; it can refer to the love toward one's child or one's parents. We can feel love toward our country or even toward certain products or activities. In all cases, the word is used to describe a positive emotion, but the nature of the feeling is very different depending on the object of love. "Kindness" is a related term. Similar to love, kindness has a positive connotation. Often, we use the adjectives "kind" and "loving" in the same sentence, such as "She is a kind and loving person." This implies that the person we are describing is a good and caring human being who is concerned about the welfare of others, empathic, socially connected to others, and compassionate.

Loving-kindness (Metta) Meditation

As you practice the following meditation, you will gently repeat some phrases, directing the compassion and acceptance they embody toward different groups of people and toward yourself. When doing this, try not to slip into just repeating them on auto-pilot mode. Instead, try to utter the phrases mindfully each time, bringing your full awareness to the phrases, their meaning, and the feelings they bring up. You can also experiment with your phrases as you go, and change them to best suit your own practice of *metta* (loving-kindness).

Let's try it. Choose four phrases from the list below or make up your own phrases. The process of choosing the phrases often helps us to clarify our intention, and you may refine and change your phrases over the course of the practice.

May you be safe

May you be happy

May you love and accept yourself just as you are

May you be free from suffering and the causes of suffering

May you be peaceful

May you be joyful

May you be courageous and joyful

May you be free from fear

May you live with ease

May your life unfold with ease

May you be wise and skillful

Again, if you can think of a better phrase yourself, use that. Whatever you feel comfortable with. Carrie, for example, chose the phrases "May you be free from fear," "May you be courageous and joyful," "May you be wise and skillful," and "May you be powerful and strong" (her own). You will be directing these phrases to various people, including yourself.

This practice should not be seen as mere mechanical repetitions of images or phrases. Rather, the goal is to mindfully investigate what happens when we generate loving-kindness and compassion to gain insight into the nature of these emotions as well as our personal relationships to them. The steps are as follows (try to spend at least five to ten minutes on each step):

1. Focus on a benefactor (i.e., a person for whom you feel strong respect and gratitude. The person should still be alive and does not invoke sexual desires).

2. Focus on a good friend (i.e., a person who is still alive and who does not invoke sexual desires).

3. Focus on self.

4. Focus on a neutral person (i.e., a person who is still alive and who does not elicit either particularly positive or negative feelings but who is commonly encountered during a normal day).

5. Focus on a "difficult" person (i.e., a person who is alive and who is associated with negative feelings).

6. Focus on the self, good friend, neutral person, and difficult person (dividing your attention equally between them).

7. Focus on groups.

The focus on the self can be quite difficult for people with SAD and depression. If it is, feel free to place this later in the sequence, such as after the neutral person.

If you don't feel any change during your meditation, don't force it. For example, in the first category, simply contemplate the benefactor and their goodness, or think of how they helped you. Then direct the metta phrases toward your benefactor. Whether or not a feeling of metta arises, you can stay connected to the phrases, their meaning, and a sense of the benefactor. Your choice of benefactor may change over time, which is fine. Try to connect to each phrase, one at a time. There is no need to worry about what has gone by or to anticipate what has not yet come, not even the next phrase. Don't struggle to manufacture a feeling of metta. Simply repeat the phrases, thereby showing your intention, and trust that nature will take its own course.

For a benefactor, Carrie considered a former colleague and friend who moved away, their doctor, and their little niece, and chose their doctor. During the practice, Carrie called the doctor to mind, visualized her, and said her name to themself. Carrie recalled different ways she had helped Carrie and others. The thought about how many people the doctor has already helped energized Carrie's positive feelings (metta) toward her.

Carrie was able to experience positive feelings toward their doctor (the benefactor) as well as toward the good friend. Next, Carrie moved on to the neutral person. When focusing on a neutral person, think for a moment about this person's place as a living being, like you, wanting to be happy just as all of us do, making mistakes just as all of us do. We have no reason to feel separate from this person. Like us, they were once children, vulnerable, limited in understanding, and dependent on the adults around them. Like us, neutral people are trying to respond to the challenges and responsibilities of adulthood in a manner that brings them happiness. They will experience both joy and sorrow. They will be both skillful and unskillful. And like us, they are subject to illness, aging, and death. When we stop and reflect on these insights, we see we have many things in common with neutral people. When we recognize these common human experiences that we share with neutral people, it is possible to feel connected and less isolated.

Just as we can wish a benefactor, ourselves, and a loved one peace, happiness, and well-being, we can wish a neutral person peace, happiness, and well-being. Try to reflect on their wish to be happy, identical to your own, and direct your metta phrases toward them for a moment. Think of them as having their own lives with ups and downs and the same uncontrollable cycle of bad and good. Carrie chose the custodian at work.

Next, Carrie moved metta toward themself. Think of life as a road with lots of unexpected twists and turns, hills and valleys. Imagine walking this road with a critical person who always finds fault with you. Perhaps this person criticizes you for being slow, for feeling lost, for stumbling and falling. Next imagine walking this same road with a kind person (the benefactor) who is understanding, friendly, and has a good sense of humor. This person cheers you on and points out what a challenge this road is and how no one gave you a map. This person congratulates you for being on the road even when you feel lost and for picking yourself up when you have fallen. This person acknowledges your strengths and uses the ups and downs on the road to help you increase your wisdom and understanding of yourself and others. This is the same road, but walking with a kind person would be very different from walking the road with a critical person. We all have an inner kind voice and inner critical voice within us. This voice keeps us company as we walk the road of life. Learning to be kind to oneself requires paying more attention to the kind voice. Note, the road stays the same. You always get the same twists and turns; the difference is how you walk it. Being kind to oneself can be difficult. We often hold ourselves to very high standards that are impossible to achieve. We then criticize ourselves for not reaching these unattainable standards. Other times there are many things we do in a day that go well and where we are skillful, but we do not pause to focus on these things and give ourselves credit. Rather, we focus on the one thing we did that was unskillful or that we feel we could have handled in a better way. We can put a lot of time and energy into criticizing ourselves for an error. We would never talk to another person in the judging way we talk to ourselves. Imagine talking to yourself as you do to a good friend.

Deliberately strengthen your kind inner kind voice in metta meditation. The inner critical voice will weaken with time. If you have a habit of finding fault and being hard on yourself, learning to be kind and friendly can take time. A range of feelings can surface, from feeling unworthy and undeserving to feeling selfish. Should you experience resistance and difficult feelings when you practice loving-kindness meditation for yourself, meet these feelings with mindfulness. In other words, observe them with acceptance and without judgment. Be curious about how you think about yourself. Carrie found the self-focus difficult, but was eventually able to focus metta on themself. The same was true for the difficult person. A difficult person is a person with whom we experience conflict, fear, or anger. It is usually best to begin with a person you find only mildly difficult—not the person who has hurt you most deeply in your life. Choose a mildly difficult person—someone you feel you can work with in your metta practice, perhaps someone who has difficult qualities but who also has qualities you can see that you appreciate. It is important to approach increasingly difficult people gradually. Trust your own wisdom and work in a way that seems beneficial to you. Carrie chose a colleague from work who was very mean to them because of Carrie's sexual orientation.

Practicing loving-kindness for a difficult person can be challenging. Extending loving-kindness to a difficult person in no way means that you permit or accept their actions.

As you practice loving-kindness for a difficult person, various thoughts and feelings will arise, possibly including sadness, anger, grief, or shame. Allow whatever arises to pass through you, holding them in kindness, without judgment. If the feelings are overwhelming, go back to practicing loving-kindness for yourself or a good friend for a while, before returning to a difficult person when you feel ready. If anger or other difficult emotions arise during loving-kindness practice for a difficult person, you may also ask yourself, *Who is the one suffering from this anger?*

Eventually the goal is to send metta equally to all living beings. However, to break open our sense of "self" and "other" and be truly open, we must first identify and focus on where these distinctions are rooted, and slowly chip away at the barriers we have created. The events of our lives often lead us to hold certain biases for or against certain groups of people. Some of these biases we are conscious of, whereas other feelings and opinions about groups of people are often outside our awareness. The practice of loving-kindness to groups of people helps to bring into awareness barriers we have erected for basic good-heartedness toward others. Bringing these feelings into awareness helps us to work with these feelings and open our hearts. In the practice of metta meditation for groups of people, you may choose a group with two categories (e.g., people you know versus people you don't know; people with SAD versus people without SAD) and work with this group using the same four loving-kindness phrases you have chosen. In practicing, you will alternate sending metta to either side of this distinction.

You may notice affinities growing for one side—this is an important part of this exploration. See where you have a tendency to exclude certain people from your metta, and focus more on genuinely including them. No one is better off if others are less happy. Think about how you behave when you're tired or stressed…we tend to be a bit more irritable and not as kind, right? Other people in the world who honk at you in traffic or even who have deeply hurt you or someone else—think about what may have led them to that place. Perhaps they just lost their job or had a painful family life growing up. There are usually reasons that people are the way they are, even if we don't know those reasons. Carrie chose the categories binary and nonbinary people.

At the end, Carrie was able to do the entire metta meditation within thirty minutes. As they sat comfortably, in a relaxed way, with closed eyes, Carrie directed their metta phrases toward a benefactor (three minutes), a neutral person, a beloved friend, a difficult person, self, and an entire group.

In the last few chapters you learned that thinking, doing, and feeling are all strongly interconnected. The way and what you think influences how you feel. Additionally, depending on what you expect from a situation, you will choose one behavior over another or choose to avoid a social situation because you expect a bad outcome. As a result, anxiety is controlling you and your life is becoming increasingly restricted. Danger seems to be everywhere.

In order to break free from the chains of SAD, you need to challenge it head on. The thinking tools we learned about in chapter 4 allow you to identify and challenge the critical inner voices that are trying to convince you of the potential danger of social situations. The only way to quiet these voices and to free yourself is to create situations that will allow you to test your predictions, as we learned in chapter 5. Will people actually laugh at me? And if so, how bad would that be? Will they be angry with me? What would they do? Will everybody notice my mishap? You will never know the answers unless you try it. And as long as you choose to stay in your cage, you will never know what a beautiful life there is outside. Go ahead, see for yourself. The door of the cage is unlocked. Open it. Step outside. You will realize that social situations are *not* dangerous. Mishaps and awkward scenarios happen often and they happen to all of us. In fact, social blunders make life more livable and people more likeable. But even more important than being liked by others is that *you* like *yourself* just the way you are—the focus of this chapter. Once you get to this point, social anxiety will have no more power over you.

Accepting yourself just the way you are and becoming less critical and kinder toward yourself is not an easy task. Metta meditation can assist in this. Using this old Buddhist practice can help you enhance your positive feelings toward your own self and others. It might seem like an odd practice. But if you find yourself being overly critical toward others and yourself, try it out. The Beatles told us that "all you need is love." But even if it's not all we need, it surely won't hurt us either.

CHAPTER 7

Bringing Down Your Arousal

Sometimes your arousal in a social situation might be very high. There are specific tools you can use to lower the arousal you experience when confronted with some social situations, especially social performance situations, such as public speaking. The tools you learn in this chapter will teach you how to reduce the high level of arousal you might be experiencing when confronted with a social threat. These tools are particularly effective to target the low perceived emotional control that is common in people with SAD (see chapter 2, figure 2: Maintenance of SAD). Experiencing a decline in your arousal will enhance your perception of emotional control. This might lead you to the insight: *I have more control over my body and my anxiety than I thought I had.*

"Face your fear" is a powerful principle to reduce any kind of irrational fear in any kind of situation. This is often easier said than done. The key is to start moving and to take one step at a time working toward your goal; as the saying goes, "Every journey begins with one first step" (often attributed to the Chinese philosopher Lao Tzu). To make it manageable, you might want to break each step into even smaller steps. You want to challenge yourself, but you don't want to discourage yourself by expecting too much of yourself. Your anxiety will eventually go down through the process of habituation after repeated and prolonged exposure to the fear-provoking situation while gaining a more adaptive perspective on the threatening situations. This is because you realize that the feared outcome is not going to happen and if it does, you can cope with it. In most cases, many different aspects of a situation induce anxiety. In social performance situations, people often report that the anxiety-related bodily sensations can easily trigger further anxiety. In fact, many people attribute most of their problems in social performance situations to the panic symptoms they experience in these situations. If you are one of those people, this tool set will be particularly helpful for dealing with performance anxiety—whether it is public speaking, sharing your opinion in a group, or just going to a party where you feel you have to perform in some way.

Strong physical sensations (such as those we have when experiencing panic) can be very frightening, especially when they happen in social situations. A panic attack is a state of intensive physiological arousal. Some people with panic attacks report (and may also show actual signs) that their heart is racing or their palms are sweating. They might also experience chest pain or shortness of breath, numbness or tingling in their arms and legs, dizziness, or light-headedness. These bodily symptoms can be frightening, although they are simply extreme forms of fear and anxiety that do not cause actual harm to the body. They are commonly experienced by people who are confronted with fear-provoking situations, including social performance tasks. They can also be experienced by people who do not have social anxiety but who fear other situations or objects, such as flying or animals. If the symptoms appear to come from out of the blue, for no apparent reason, this may be a sign of a condition known as panic disorder. Of course, some people can have both, panic disorder and social anxiety disorder, as well as other problems.

Regardless of the nature of your panic attacks or strong physiological arousal, the thinking tools you learned in chapter 4 to target probability overestimation, catastrophic thinking, and other thinking errors can help you realize that those attacks do not cause any actual bodily harm and do not have any other long-lasting and irreversible consequences. Specifically, you might be concerned that other people notice your panic symptoms and therefore judge you negatively. But remember that chances are probably quite low that people notice (targeting probability overestimation) and even if they do, most wouldn't care much (targeting catastrophic thinking). Still, the sensations can be quite intense and can demand your attention, enhancing your self-focused attention and moving your attentional resources away from the task at hand.

Let's go back to our first driving lesson and experience the anxiety it evoked. First, turn the key to start the engine while keeping your foot on the break, then look over your shoulder and check your mirror, and then release the foot from the break and gently push down on the gas pedal. Too hard. More gently! All of this demanded a great deal of your attentional resources at the beginning. But now that you have become a pro, you can listen to the radio while talking to your spouse in the passenger seat and while watching your kids in the rearview mirror, trying to make them stop fighting. And you do all this while flying down a four-lane highway scanning the road for highway patrol. What a difference! The simple act of "overlearning" (i.e., doing one thing over and over and over again) frees up attentional resources by forming habits and by turning a new sequence of behaviors into an automatic set of actions. The obvious consequence of this habit formation is that the fear of operating a motor vehicle all but disappeared. The same is true for social performance tasks: the more often you do it, the easier and more habitual it becomes, and the less anxiety you will experience. If you failed you driver's test a few times because your anxiety interfered with satisfactory task performance, you probably should have listened to your friend who told you to relax and calm down. Again, the same applies to social performance tasks. If your anxiety is simply too intense to deal with the task, then try to lower the temperature by practicing some simple relaxation skills.

In essence, there are two principal strategies to deal with strong physiological (i.e., bodily) arousal, such as panic symptoms. Prior to confronting the panic-inducing situation, you may repeatedly expose yourself to the sensations in order to habituate to them, making it less likely that they will bother you when you are in the social situation. We call this technique *interoceptive habituation exercises*. Alternatively, you may use arousal reduction techniques such as relaxation exercises. We'll start with the first strategy.

Interoceptive Habituation Exercises

These exercises are intended for you to repeatedly confront yourself with unpleasant arousal sensations prior to entering the feared social situation. Let me illustrate this. Please put down the book for a minute, stand up, and breathe through your mouth, very forcefully, in and out very fast (about one in-out cycle per second). Do this for about one minute. How are you feeling now? Typically, people feel dizzy and light-headed, might have a dry mouth, have a racing heart and maybe sweaty palms. Does this list sound familiar? Well, these are some of the very same bodily experiences we have when we experience intense fear or panic. For this reason, you might have also felt discomfort or even anxiety. This is because this exercise triggers the very same physiological system that is activated during states of intense fear. Because you brought it on yourself by breathing very hard, your fear response is probably not as intense as it would have been if you had experienced these sensations when doing a social performance task.

As you are reading these lines, your symptoms have probably vanished. The same is true for physiological sensations you experience with social fears. Eventually, your physical sensations decrease and lose their ability to trigger or enhance your anxiety in the social performance situation. Initially, it might take some time for your anxiety to come down. It depends on the specific situation, your history, and many other factors. But I promise you that eventually, your anxiety will come down.

Breathing in particular is key for this. Our little exercise demonstrates that breathing has a direct effect on your anxiety: Breathing too much can cause anxiety; slowing down your breathing can calm you down when you are anxious. Of course, breathing alone is not going to cure your anxiety. But it will help. One reason for this is that breathing is directly linked to a particular branch of your autonomic nervous system, the parasympathetic nervous system, and its primary nerve, the vagus nerve. Activation of the vagus nerve has many health benefits, ranging from lowering blood pressure and heart rate to lowering depression and anxiety. We know that slow breathing activates the vagus nerve and that people with anxiety problems often show inflexibility or low activation of the vagus nerve. Therefore, the way we breathe has a significant effect on our body (especially our heart) and our feeling of anxiety.

It might surprise you that breathing is so important in addressing anxiety because we rarely notice our breathing; and yet it's something we easily control. The normal rate of breathing is about ten to fifteen breaths per minute. When we breathe, we take in oxygen from the air and breathe out carbon dioxide (our metabolism turns oxygen and sugar into carbon dioxide and energy). When we perform strenuous physical activity, such as aerobic exercise, we breathe faster and deeper because our body requires more oxygen as our metabolism increases. In contrast to many other bodily functions, our breathing is under our voluntary control. If we breathe faster and deeper without performing a strenuous physical activity, we bring more oxygen into our blood and decrease the level of carbon dioxide beyond our body's needs. This is also referred to as "hyperventilation." If the extra amount of oxygen is not used up at the rate at which it is brought in, we experience a number of characteristic changes: light-headedness, dizziness, dry mouth, tingling in the arms and hands, and becoming flushed.

What would happen if you experienced the same symptoms in a real social performance situation (e.g., when giving a public speech)? Imagine you voluntarily hyperventilated right before you went on stage, ready to give a speech in front of people. Imagine having the same symptoms you had during our hyperventilation exercise earlier. As you know, these symptoms are pretty uncomfortable by themselves, so imagine how much more uncomfortable they would be when exposed to a social threat, such as when standing on stage. Some people, especially those who are bothered by those bodily sensations, might interpret this as extreme anxiety and panic. In fact, breathing too fast and too deeply can cause physical sensations that can further increase your anxiety in the social situation. You don't need to be concerned about passing out when hyperventilating. You might feel very dizzy and as if you are passing out, but it's close to impossible to make yourself pass out by hyperventilating. So, as an interoceptive habituation exercise, you might try hyperventilating a few times to experience the uncomfortable sensations. You can combine this with imaginal exposures, where you imagine yourself being confronted with a threating situation.

Aside from hyperventilation, there are a number of other bodily sensations that some people find fear-producing when combined with an imaginal exposure practice. Below is a list of some easy one-minute exercises that induce different bodily sensations:

Exercise	Symptoms/Experience
Hyperventilation	Shortness of breath, dizziness
Head shaking	Dizziness
Running in place	Heart racing
Breath holding	Chest tightness
Body tensing	Trembling
Spinning	Dizziness
Looking into a mirror	Feelings of unreality

As we would expect, hyperventilation causes the most intense sensations. But other exercises can also be useful because they induce different feelings that might be more anxiety-producing for you than the strong sensations during hyperventilation.

If you have a serious medical condition that limits the physical activity you can perform safely (e.g., a heart condition or epilepsy), please consult with your doctor before you do these exercises. If you can go to a gym regularly or can still go for a run, you probably do not need to worry about any of these exercises. But better safe than sorry.

People are different, and, as we already discussed, some people are more concerned about bodily sensations during social performance situations than others, and some sensations are distressing for some but not for others. Much of your success will therefore depend on your ability to be creative and modify the techniques so they fit your personal needs. You might wonder how this relates to your social anxiety. Well, none of these exercises specifically target social anxiety. Rather, these exercises induce symptoms that some people with social anxiety strongly dislike, often because they happen when they feel panicky in social situations. As you are doing these exercises and are getting some of these unpleasant sensations, similar to the feeling you have in social situations, you should focus on those sensations.

Table 6 shows Joseph's experience doing those exercises while imagining himself in an anxiety-producing social performance situation (i.e., imaginal exposure). As you can see, he rated the intensity of both his symptoms and his anxiety while performing each exercise.

Table 6: Joseph's Fear Induction Exercises

Exercise	Symptoms/Experience	Intensity of Symptoms (0–8)	Intensity of Anxiety (0–8)
Hyperventilation	Shortness of breath, dizziness	6	6
Head shaking	Dizziness	3	2
Running in place	Heart racing	5	4
Breath holding	Chest tightness	1	0
Body tensing	Trembling	6	4
Spinning	Dizziness	4	2
Looking into a mirror	Feelings of unreality	1	0

For Joseph, hyperventilating, body tensing, and running in place created the greatest degree of anxiety in conjunction with the imaginal exposure script. He would need to repeatedly do these exercises to desensitize himself to these physical manifestations of his anxiety and decrease his fear of these symptoms. He started out by tensing his body. Joseph did this exercise daily, five times in a row, until his anxiety decreased to a mild level (2) more quickly. He then did the same exercise while imagining a threatening social performance situation. He did this a number of times until his anxiety was at a mild level. Then, he moved on to running in place, and then hyperventilating, all while imagining the social performance situation. He targeted hyperventilating last because initially it had created the greatest anxiety. In each case, his anxiety came down after only a few days of repeated practice. Only his anxiety when hyperventilating while imagining the fearful scene took a little longer to decline. Table 7 shows his hyperventilation exercise on three consecutive days. As you can see, hyperventilation elicited intense bodily symptoms every time he did this. (Unless you modify the task from one trial to the next, you should expect the same intensity of bodily sensations.) However, his emotional response to these sensations (i.e., the intensity of anxiety) gradually deceased from one trial to the next.

Table 7: Joseph's Repeated Exposure to Fearful Sensations Practice Trials

Date/Time	Exercise	Practice Trials	Intensity of Symptoms (0–8)	Intensity of Anxiety (0–8)
8/26/22 6 p.m.	Hyperventilating	1	6	5
		2	6	5
		3	7	4
		4	6	3
		5	7	3
8/27/22 5 p.m.		1	5	4
		2	5	3
		3	5	3
		4	5	2
8/28/22 6 p.m.		1	6	3
		2	6	2
		3	6	2

At this point, Joseph might want to do these exercises while imaging a threating social situation. He may choose to begin with a mildly threatening situation first (such as meeting new people) and then move up to more threatening ones, such as public speaking. Gradually, these bodily symptoms will lose their power over him and will lead to little or no anxiety. He will then also be able to confront real social situations with less trepidation, and his attention won't be drawn away from the situation toward his sensations and his anxiety. Again, this will not work for everybody, but it might work for you. So try it out. (You can find blank copies of tables 6 and 7 at http://www.newharbinger.com/51208.)

Relaxation Exercise

Including relaxation exercises in the arsenal of techniques to fight social performance anxiety may seem odd based on what we've covered so far. Aren't relaxation techniques also strategies to avoid facing one's fear? Don't these techniques also lead us into an avoidance cycle that can be difficult to break? Isn't the goal to accept rather than to suppress anxiety or artificially lower it? The answer is "yes, but." There are some exceptions. In some occasions, the anticipatory anxiety can be so intense and overwhelming that it feels impossible to confront the actual situation. If you know which sensations make you feel very uncomfortable in social situations, do the practices we discussed to desensitize yourself. But if, despite all your best effort, the sensations come over you, feel overwhelming, and engulf you, there is something you can do. One useful, easy, established, and effective relaxation technique is progressive muscle relaxation (PMR), which was developed in the 1960s. This exercise involves tensing the muscles in each major muscle group, followed by releasing the tension and relaxing. This two-step process will allow you to achieve the deepest level of muscle relaxation. First, you apply *tension* to your muscles for a brief amount of time. Second, you *relax* that muscle group for a slightly longer amount of time. The overall goal of PMR is to learn how to relax the whole body at once, but first I'll give you instructions on each step.

Before we dive into PMR, it's important to distinguish between two types of applied tension. The first type is called *active tensing*. This type of tension occurs when you are purposefully trying to tense a particular muscle group as hard as you can without hurting yourself. PMR often starts with using active tensing for isolated muscle groups. After practice, you can use it for multiple muscle groups at the same time, and eventually the whole body. In general, active tensing is the standard type of tension you use while practicing PMR. The second type of tension is called *passive tensing*. Unlike active tensing, passive tensing involves merely noticing whatever tensions already exist in a particular muscle group. That is, you are not purposefully attempting to apply tension. Although active tensing is often preferred because it usually leads to greater relaxation, there might be some circumstances in which you want to consider passive tensing. In particular, passive tensing is often recommended for muscles or regions of your body that have suffered an injury or are in pain. It's important not to cause further injury to any part of your body, which makes passive tensing a worthwhile alternative. With passive tensing, you note the tension that exists in a muscle area and then focus greater efforts on the relaxation phase.

For this exercise, you'll want to use a prompt, which is any verbal phrase or mantra that invokes the idea of deep relaxation (e.g., "relax"). This could include concepts such as heaviness, sleepiness, or calmness. The relaxation phase will always be longer than the tension phase. In general, you should tense your muscles for a relatively short amount of time, and then take a longer period of time to allow yourself to enter into a state of deep relaxation. Don't give in to the temptation to quickly pass over the relaxation phase just to move on to the next muscle group! You'd be selling yourself short of getting the best benefits from PMR. It's important to have patience when it comes to this exercise. If you move too quickly from muscle group to muscle group, you might end up feeling more stressed out! So please, take your time, and allow yourself to experience deep relaxation. There is no rush.

I will describe here the twelve-muscle-group PMR. (You can also download this exercise from the website for this book, http://www.newharbinger.com/51208.) The idea is to first practice it repeatedly under calm, nonstressful situations. Once you have learned this and feel comfortable with it, you may shorten it to just eight muscle groups (by combining some of the muscle groups), then four, then two. Eventually, you'll have the goal of relaxing very quickly with just one step when confronted with a stressful situation in order to lower your level of arousal. To practice PMR, pick a quiet space with a comfortable chair or bed. When positioning yourself, please sit in an upright posture, and make sure you have enough space in front of you to move your arms and legs. Initially, you should choose a place that's not distracting. Make sure to wear loose clothing and remove glasses or contact lenses. The practice will take about twenty to thirty minutes, so make sure you are able to set aside time for this during the day.

Come up with your prompt and say it to yourself while practicing. I'll use the word "relax" for the purpose of this exercise, but use whatever prompt you'd like. Remember not to use active tension on any muscle groups or areas of your body that are injured. Consider skipping that injured muscle or using passive tension for that muscle instead. Here are the steps.

1. Close your eyes and relax. Take some deep breaths from your belly as you sit quietly.

2. Produce tension in your lower arms by making fists and pulling up on your wrists so that your wrists nearly touch your shoulders.

    a. Focus on the tension (10 seconds).

    b. Now release the tension in your lower arms and hands. Let your arms relax with your palms down. Relax your muscles and focus your attention on the feeling of relaxation (50 seconds).

    c. Continue to breathe deeply and think the word "relax" with each exhale.

3. Produce tension in your upper arms by leaning forward, pulling your arms back and in to the sides of your body, and trying to touch your elbows behind your back.

    a. Focus on the tension (10 seconds).

b.   Now release your arms and relax (50 seconds), letting all the tension go. Feel the difference between the tension and the relaxation.

c.   As you sit quietly, say the word "relax."

4.   Produce tension in your lower legs by flexing your feet up and bringing your toes toward your upper body, trying to touch your toes to your knees.

a.   Feel the tension in your feet, ankles, shins, and calves. Focus on the tension (10 seconds).

b.   Now release the tension and feel the difference between the tension and the relaxation (50 seconds).

c.   As you sit quietly, think the word "relax" with each exhale from your belly.

5.   Produce tension in your upper legs by bringing your knees together and lifting your legs off the chair.

a.   Focus on the tension in your upper legs (10 seconds).

b.   Now, release the tension in your legs and feel the difference between the tension and the relaxation. Focus on the feeling of relaxation (50 seconds).

c.   Think the word "relax" as you continue to sit quietly, breathing deeply.

6.   Produce tension in your stomach by pulling your stomach tightly in toward your spine.

a.   Feel the tension and tightness; focus on that part of your body (10 seconds).

b.   Now let your stomach go and relax outward. Feel the comfortable feeling of relaxation (50 seconds).

c.   As you sit quietly, think the word "relax" with each exhale.

7.   Produce tension around your chest by taking a deep breath and holding it.

a.   Feel the tension in your chest and back. Hold your breath (10 seconds).

b.   Now relax, let the air out slowly (50 seconds), and feel the difference between the tension and the relaxation.

c.   As you sit quietly, continuing to breathe deeply, think the word "relax."

8. Produce tension in your shoulders by bringing your shoulders up toward your ears.

   a. Focus on the tension in your shoulders and neck (10 seconds).

   b. Now drop your shoulders; let them droop and relax. Concentrate on the sensation of relaxation (50 seconds).

   c. As you sit quietly, think the word "relax."

9. Produce tension around your neck by tilting your chin down and trying to press the back of your neck against the chair or toward the wall behind you.

   a. Focus on the tightness around the back of your neck (10 seconds).

   b. Now release the tension and concentrate on the relaxation (50 seconds). and feel the difference between the tension and the relaxation.

   c. As you sit quietly, think the word "relax" with each deep exhale.

10. Produce tension around your mouth and jaw by clenching your teeth and pushing the corners of your mouth back.

    a. Feel the tension in your mouth and jaw (10 seconds).

    b. Now release the tension, allowing your mouth to drop open, and concentrate on the difference between the tension and the relaxation (50 seconds).

    c. As you sit quietly, think the word "relax."

11. Produce tension around your eyes by tightly squeezing your eyes shut (3 seconds).

    a. Feel the tension around your eyes (10 seconds).

    b. Now release the tension in your eyes, and feel the difference between the tension and the relaxation (50 seconds).

    c. As you sit quietly, continuing to breathe deeply from your belly, think the word "relax."

12. Produce tension across your lower forehead by pulling your eyebrows down toward the center of your face and frowning.

    a. Focus on the tension in your forehead (10 seconds).

    b. Now relax your forehead and feel the difference between the tension and the relaxation (50 seconds).

    c. Think the word "relax" with each exhale.

13. Produce tension in your upper forehead by raising your eyebrows to the top of your head.

    a. Focus on the pulling sensation and tension across your forehead (10 seconds).

    b. Now relax your eyebrows and focus on the difference between the tension and the relaxation.

    c. As you sit quietly, think the word "relax."

14. You are fully relaxed. Continue to sit quietly with your eyes closed and breathing deeply from your belly. Count to yourself from one to five, making yourself feel more and more relaxed.

    a. One, allow all of the tension to leave your body.

    b. Two, feel yourself dropping further and further down into relaxation.

    c. Three, you're feeling more and more relaxed.

    d. Four, you're feeling quite relaxed.

    e. Five, you're feeling completely relaxed.

    f. As you're in this relaxed state, focus on all of your muscles being completely comfortable and stress free.

    g. As you sit in this state, breathing deeply, think the word "relax" with each deep exhale (2 minutes).

15. Now, focus on counting backward from five and feeling yourself becoming more alert.

    a. Five, you're feeling more alert.

    b. Four, you're feeling yourself coming out of the relaxation state.

    c. Three, you're feeling more awake.

    d. Two, you're opening your eyes.

    e. One, you're sitting up and feeling completely awake and alert.

I could have discussed a number of different relaxation techniques. Autogenic training, diaphragmatic breathing, and visualization are just some of the techniques you may use as an alternative. Some exercises require some time to learn and patience to practice (such as autogenic training). PMR is relatively easy, and you can quickly apply it in a stressful situation. Plus, as an added bonus, you might even expand your life expectancy by a few years by reducing your overall stress level. But make sure you don't use it as an avoidance strategy. Use it only in situations when you feel like your arousal is too high to deal with in an adaptive way. Consider PMR, or other relaxation techniques, as a safety valve that turns on when the temperature is too high, to let out some steam and bring the temperature down a bit. Not everybody will need to use these techniques. Use them only if you believe that your arousal is too high and getting in the way of applying other strategies, such as the thinking tools described earlier. Try them out and stick to the tools that work well for you. No mechanic can fix a car with a single screwdriver. It requires a set of tools. One size fits all might work for socks, but not for tools to deal with SAD.

CHAPTER 8

Improving Your Social Skills

Although many people with SAD believe that their social skills are deficient, the vast majority of people with SAD have adequate social skills. However, a small group of people with SAD do exhibit obvious problems with social skills that often can be easily corrected. Some people avoid eye contact, speak too quietly, or show distracting stereotypic behaviors, verbal fillers, or gestures. Others may even confuse assertiveness with aggression. If you are one of these people, improving your social skills can be helpful to correct these obvious distractions and problems. Social performance of any kind requires some social skills, and anxiety can negatively affect your social skills, which can then lead to even greater anxiety. The goal of this chapter is not to turn you into a perfectly skilled social performer. Instead, these tools are intended to correct some easily correctible social skills issues that can get in the way of your social encounters.

In the 1990s, the late Samuel Turner, his close collaborator Deborah Beidel, and their colleagues developed and tested a treatment for social anxiety called social effectiveness therapy (Turner et al. 1994). This treatment, which included social skills trainings in the context of exposure therapy and CBT, was quite effective for treating SAD. Based on the evidence, it appears, however, that the improvements were primarily due to the exposure techniques rather than to learning new social skills. Despite having good or adequate social skills, most people with social anxiety—perhaps you included—*believe* that their social skills are very poor and therefore feel inadequate and awkward in certain social situations. In fact, social anxiety and social skills are not closely associated at all, and I have seen many non-anxious people who believe that their social skills are very good, even though they are not. Still, correcting some very specific and easily changeable social skills problems you might have, such as avoiding eye contact or speaking too softly, can be a very helpful tool in your tool box to deal with SAD.

Context Sensitivity and Flexibility

Perhaps the most important social skill is the ability to flexibly adjust your behavior to a given context and to the changing demands of a given situation. For this reason, there is no skill that is always right no matter the context. It always depends. The context determines what is appropriate and what is inappropriate. Being loud is inappropriate in most settings. But sometimes, being loud is appropriate, such as during a football match. It just depends. We learn those rules through our culture and socialization, and we can adopt new rules or modify old rules quite easily as we experience different cultures or settings. This means, however, that every skill we consider here is always context dependent and simply a rule of thumb. Talking quietly and staring into somebody's eyes seem inappropriate most of the time but might be appropriate when comforting and consoling your friend during moments of grief and sadness.

A concrete example of context insensitivity and inflexibility occurred during one of our experiments at Stanford. For this particular study, my students and I recruited people who feel very little anxiety when giving a speech in front of people (which is not very common). One of the participants was a successful and very friendly businessman who had moved from a non-English speaking country to the US only months before this experiment. Being a non-native English speaker myself, I have the greatest sympathy for people who struggle with the English language. But this particular gentleman was more than simply struggling with the English language. When I asked him to give a ten-minute speech about a certain topic, my colleagues and I were unable to understand a single word of what he was saying. In fact, we first thought he gave the speech in a different language.

But after carefully listening to his recordings again, we were actually able to make out some English words and phrases. Surprisingly, this gentleman reported no distress whatsoever, and also showed no bodily signs of anxiety as measured with sophisticated psychophysiological equipment. In fact, it was apparent that he greatly enjoyed himself during the experiment.

What makes this story so amusing? The businessman seemed completely insensitive to the given context. He was unfazed by the fact that his English was inadequate for the task and context (i.e., to give a speech in English). Moreover, he seemed to lack the insight of his own language problems and did not appreciate the perspective of others (i.e., us, who were trying to understand what he was saying). In other words, he lacked context sensitivity and exhibited inflexibility in his approach to the task.

Interactional Skills

Interactional skills can be formal or informal. Formal interactional skills are those certain rules you need to follow, for example, introducing one person to another ("Hi, Peter, I would like you to meet Paul") or asking somebody out on a date ("Can I take you to dinner sometime?"). These rules are greatly influenced by context, such as the culture, the setting, and tradition. Growing up in Germany, I found it initially quite challenging to learn the implicit rules of the art of dating. My generation in Germany had few (if any) rules around dating. The first kiss could happen almost anytime— during the first encounter at a party or after months of friendship. Whether you were meeting somebody for lunch, dinner, or coffee was not of great importance. But it was a different experience for me when I moved to the US. For starters, there is not even a direct German translation of the phrase "Do you want to go out with me sometime?" Asking somebody to go out for dinner is a bigger deal than asking somebody for lunch, which is yet a bigger deal than asking somebody out for coffee. Little did I know. As I was learning and violating some unwritten rules, my friends would try to gently steer me clear of social mishaps. Still, I fell into some of the dating traps (sounds like a good title for another book!). I eventually learned that going out for dinner is more than ingesting calories together, that the number of times you eat dinner together is meaningful, that calling somebody up right after a date is undesirable, that the third dinner tends to be more personal than the second, and that saying, "I will call you," and then not, usually means that the dating game is over. If you are accustomed to US culture, you know what I am talking about. But if you are coming from another culture, you might not understand some of the issues I just mentioned.

Below I'll talk about a few key aspects of positive interactional skills.

Kindness and Empathy

Most of us like nice people and try to distance ourselves from those who are rude. Rude people can still be successful, depending on your definition of "success." I could name many politicians and dictators who are rude and successful because they achieved what they wanted to in terms of wealth, power, and dominance. But if you define "success" as being liked by others, rude people will not be on the short list of the most likeable people.

It is not hard to list the characteristics of a rude person, such as one who is selfish, aggressive, and violates other people's personal space. More difficult is the concept of kindness. If we all knew what it is, it would be a nicer world. Kindness is related to empathy, genuineness, and unconditional positive regard. These are the three pillars of Carl Rogers's client-centered therapy, which is the foundation of humanistic therapy (Rogers 1951). This has become an essential therapeutic context for virtually every talking therapy, and these three pillars are also the essential features of any close interpersonal relationship.

Empathy is the ability to understand and experience another person's feelings. Genuineness means being authentic and sincere. Unconditional positive regard means accepting and supporting the other person, no matter what they are saying or doing. These three qualities create a safe and non-judgmental environment for relationships to thrive. Any interpersonal interaction can quickly be enhanced if you show empathy, genuineness, and unconditional positive regard toward the other person.

Humor, Reciprocity, Eye Contact, and Gestures

Most of us tend to like other people if they make us feel good. Humor, whether intended or unintended, is a powerful agent to reduce stress and improve the quality of an interaction. Spilling your glass of water at a dinner table can be embarrassing, but it can also provide an opportunity for humor, especially if it's self-deprecating humor. But be careful making fun of others. You are judged as more likeable when you can laugh at yourself, not at others. As is true for all of these skills, there are often cultural differences. Of note, the word *schadenfreude*—meaning getting enjoyment from other people's troubles—appears to be unique to the German language.

Social interaction is a give-and-take. It should not be one-sided. This is also called *social reciprocity*. This means that all things being equal, both people have similar speaking time. If one person has a story to tell, the storyteller will obviously spend more time talking than the listener. But if this person has many stories to tell, it becomes a one-sided relationship that is typically less appreciated by the listener than the speaker. In contrast, asking questions signals interest and is a good conversation starter. It also enables the conversation to get more into details and become more meaningful. However, asking too many questions and even bombarding the person with seemingly unrelated questions can be exhausting for the other person. It's totally okay to stay with silence for some time.

We have discussed in previous chapters the importance of eye contact in social interactions. A brief glance can signal approval, attraction, disagreement, anger, disapproval, and so on. A look into your lover's eyes is quite different from a stare into your opponent's eyes. We look into another person's eyes in order to read their emotions. Avoiding eye contact can signal submissiveness or dislike, while long and intensive eye contact can appear threatening. Therefore, eye contact is highly context dependent, and the duration and intensity needs to be appropriate to the situation. Additionally, your gestures and body posture should somewhat match your verbal behavior; for example, you don't want to appear happy when discussing something sad, and vice versa. Gesturing and body posture should ideally emphasize what you are saying verbally. Avoid stereotypic or distracting behaviors, such as rhythmic movement of your head, rocking, twitching, or frequently crossing your legs.

Being assertive when appropriate is often appreciated, but avoid extreme displays of dominance, such as staring at a person, speaking very loudly, or interrupting the other person. This often comes across as being hostile and aggressive and is rarely adaptive and successful. Likewise, avoid extreme displays of submissiveness, such as avoiding someone's gaze or excessively apologizing, which is a common safety behavior that is not only ineffective but also quite annoying to most people. So if you find yourself saying "I'm sorry" a lot, try to make sure an apology is truly in order before you give one.

Social Performance Skills

The DSM-5 introduced a new subtype of SAD called "performance subtype." The reason for this was to capture some of the heterogeneity of the SAD diagnosis. Some people fear and/or avoid a range of different social situations, whereas some primarily fear and/or avoid social performance situations. The most common social performance situation is public speaking, so here we'll discuss some skills to help in this area.

The most important aspect of a performance—your violin or dance recital, your speech—is its quality. A good speech, for example, captures the audience's interest, moves people, and stimulates their thinking. Every speech should have an introduction, a middle part, and an end. In the introduction, a good speaker may say something to grab the audience's attention (e.g., a joke, a strong statement) and tell the audience what the talk will be about. In the middle, of course, a good speaker covers the main points about the topic, with supporting details. At the end, a good speaker summarizes the talk and often solicits questions from the audience.

If you're giving a speech or presentation, be familiar with the setting. Try to get some information about the audience in order to tailor your talk to the listeners. You may also greet some of the audience members as they arrive. You may be surprised to learn that these are people just like you and me, which may increase your comfort level.

If you give a presentation with a question and answer period at the end, you might be confronted with difficult and even hostile questions. If the questioner has a valid point, repeat and extract their main point by rephrasing it in neutral (and not hostile) language. If the question is unreasonable, tell the questioner that you would be more than happy to talk with them in person after the speech. If you feel too angry or defensive to deal with it, you may simply ignore the question and elicit other questions from the audience. Don't insult or attack the questioner. Such a behavior is typically not appreciated by the rest of the audience, no matter how hostile the question was. If for some reason you have to respond to the question (maybe because the questioner is the vice president of your company), you may say something like "Thank you very much. This is a very good question. Unfortunately, there is no simple answer to it..."

In conclusion, most people with SAD believe that they are deficient in their social skills. However, in all likelihood, your social skills are just fine. But if your social skills are, in fact, lacking, you can easily correct them. This chapter gave you some pointers. Try them out if there is good reason to assume that you have social skills deficits (e.g., if good friends mentioned something to you). Don't trust yourself to judge your own social skills. You might just be your own worst critic; good friends tend to be better judges.

Epilogue

We have reached the end after covering a lot of ground. In chapter 1, we discussed various dimensions of social anxiety and the nature of its clinical expression, social anxiety disorder. In chapter 2, you learned the many reasons why social anxiety is such a persistent problem. In chapter 3, I presented and discussed a comprehensive maintenance model and discussed why exposure is so crucial for overcoming social anxiety. The material discussed in these early chapters is based on the vast literature of scientific studies that have been conducted by many experts from around the world. These studies answered a lot of questions about social anxiety. In fact, we know a great deal about what maintains this pervasive problem. This allowed researchers to develop very specific intervention strategies, which I summarized in this book.

No two people are alike. Sarah, Joseph, and Carrie were just three examples to illustrate how social anxiety is expressed differently in different people. Social anxiety is not a monolith. This means that there is no single "thing" called "social anxiety," "social anxiety disorder," or "social phobia." Rather, there are almost as many forms of social anxiety, and how it presents itself, as there are people struggling with it. The same is true for clinical expression (*social anxiety disorder*, formerly known as *social phobia*). Fortunately, there are some notable commonalities among people, and the same strategies will help a lot of people with slightly different problems. Still, to be most effective, you need to tailor the strategies to your specific situation. I hope this book helps you find effective ways to do that.

I discussed many skills and tools you may use to deal with your social anxiety: tools to identify your thinking errors (chapter 4), tools to confront yourself with social mishaps (chapter 5), and tools to accept yourself (chapter 6). Some of these tools, such as performing social mishap exposures to examine the feared consequences, will likely benefit most, if not all, people with social anxiety. Other tools, such as those to reduce your arousal (chapter 7) or to enhance your social skills (chapter 8) will likely be more effective for some than for others. You probably have a sense of what will most likely help you the most. But if in doubt, try them all out. And if you find something hard to do, you are on the right track. You'll find a quiz to check how much you learned at http://www.newharbinger.com/51208. If your answers are off, go back to the respective chapters and re-read them. We covered a lot of information, and you can't expect to remember everything right away.

In order to effectively use these tools to free yourself from social anxiety, you will need to adopt a mindset to open yourself up to new experiences. This will entail exposing yourself to certain uncomfortable situations. It is not easy to overcome social anxiety. If there were an easier way, I would have told you about it. Sometimes, we have to endure some short-term emotional pain in order to gain peace and happiness in the long term. I admire your courage. Remember Franklin D. Roosevelt's 1933 presidential address as he faced the terror of the Third Reich: "You have nothing to fear but fear itself." The only way to overcome your fear is to confront it head on with the tools described in this book. I wish you all the best on your road to recovery.

Medications for Social Anxiety

I am not a medical doctor. I am a PhD psychologist. Therefore, you should talk to your physician for medical advice. But this book would be incomplete without a brief acknowledgment of psychiatric medications for SAD. Medications can reduce anxiety states, including social anxiety. But in my opinion, they should not be your first choice of treatment. Pharmaceutical companies have been aggressively advertising medication for SAD, such as Paxil (paroxetine) since 1999, when the Food and Drug Administration (FDA) approved it for the treatment of social phobia (now called social anxiety disorder). There are also a number of other medications available, which I will briefly discuss here. These medications form different drug classes because they differ in their actions.

To date, the most commonly used classes of medications for social anxiety include beta-blockers, monoamine oxidase inhibitors (MAOIs), and selective serotonin reuptake inhibitors (SSRIs). Other medications are also prescribed (such as tricyclic and other antidepressants), but clinical trials suggest that these medications are not overly effective in reducing social anxiety. Clinical trials typically compare the effects of various medications directly to one another and to a placebo pill, which is a sugar pill that contains no active ingredients but looks and tastes just like the real pill.

Beta-blockers, such as propranolol or atenolol, lower physiological arousal and are often used to treat high blood pressure or cardiac problems. In the past, many physicians thought that beta-blockers were also effective for treating social performance anxiety by blocking the peripheral autonomic response to the anxiety-provoking stimulus. Therefore, these drugs have been widely used for treating performance anxiety since the 1970s. Despite early enthusiasm for beta-blockers to treat social anxiety, its efficacy has not been supported by later clinical research. These drugs can be useful to lessen the physiological and behavioral components of fear (such as the heart pounding and shaking), but they have little effect on the experience of anxiety.

Many studies have shown that phenelzine, an MAOI, was significantly more effective in treating social anxiety than the beta-blocker atenolol and placebo. One study compared the effects of phenelzine, CBT, and their combination (Blanco et al. 2010). Combined phenelzine and CBT was superior to either treatment alone and to placebo on dimensional measures and on rates of response (and remission). The study reported response rates 47.1% after CBT, 54.3% after phenelzine, and 71.9% after the combination treatment. This was one of the few studies showing better effects after a combination treatment than a single form of therapy. It should be noted, however, that the CBT protocol that was used in this study was based on an earlier, more traditional version of CBT, which did not include many of the strategies described here, including the social mishap exposures. Still, these results showed that phenelzine can be an effective treatment for some patients. Unfortunately, taking phenelzine requires people to closely watch their diet, because eating certain foods (such as aged cheese) while being on this medication can cause serious physical problems (such as a hypertensive crisis).

The promising results of the studies that used MAOIs for the treatment of social anxiety stimulated research on other antidepressants with better tolerability as potential treatments for social anxiety. Since the FDA approved Paxil (paroxetine) for the treatment of social phobia in 1999, many studies have examined the efficacy of this class of medication. A recent meta-analysis of pharmacotherapies (medication treatment) recommended paroxetine as a first-line treatment of SAD (Williams et al. 2020) because, except for paroxetine, the differences between drugs and placebo were small. In contrast to phenelzine, paroxetine does not require patients to follow a strict diet. However, it can cause sexual dysfunction in some people.

 Do you personally need medication for your SAD? This is impossible to say without knowing your personal story. If you practice the techniques outlined in this book, and keep practicing these strategies, you can probably overcome your social anxiety without medication. Moreover, taking a pill as a quick fix of your social anxiety comes with a price: there are often unpleasant side effects, withdrawal symptoms, dietary restrictions, and at times even dependence when used for a longer period of time. In some cases, however, medication can be a useful intervention, especially if other problems interfere with treatment, such as depression and other psychological disorders. However, most people do not find medication helpful or necessary as long as the strategies outlined in this book work well.

 Finally, I should note that my colleagues and I have examined a particular drug called d-cycloserine (an antibiotic), which appears to speed up the treatment gains of the exposure procedures in CBT for SAD (e.g., Hofmann et al. 2013). In this study, we randomly assigned 169 patients with SAD to receive either a very small dose of this medication (50 mg) or a placebo one hour before each of five exposure sessions that were part of a twelve-session CBT group treatment. This treatment included many of the same strategies discussed in this book. The results showed that both CBT plus d-cycloserine and CBT plus placebo were associated with similar completion rates (87% and 82%) and response rates (79.3% and 73.3%) at the posttreatment assessment and were largely maintained at the follow-up assessments. D-cycloserine by itself has no effect on anxiety (it is not an anxiolytic drug). Its therapeutic effect is only present in conjunction with CBT. Because CBT resulted in a response rate of 70%–80% in both conditions, the medication had no added benefit on the response. However, it was associated with a 24%–33% faster rate of improvement in symptom severity relative to placebo during the treatment phase. This might open up new roads for pharmacotherapy: further enhancing what we know works already (i.e., CBT).

References

Alden, L. E., K. W. Auyeung, and L. Plasencia. 2014. "Social Anxiety and the Self." In *Social Anxiety: Clinical, Developmental, and Social Perspectives* (3rd edition), edited by S. G. Hofmann and P. M. DiBartolo, 513–549. Amsterdam Elsevier/Academic Press. ISBN-13: 978-0123944276.

American Psychiatric Association. 1980. *Diagnostic and Statistical Manual of Mental Disorders* (3rd edition). Washington, D.C.: APA.

American Psychiatric Association. 2013. *Diagnostic and Statistical Manual of Mental Disorders* (5th edition). Washington, D.C.: APA.

Bandura, A. 1988. "Self-Efficacy Conception of Anxiety." *Anxiety Research* 1: 77–98.

Barlow, D. H. 2001. *Anxiety and Its Disorders* (2nd edition). New York: Guilford Press.

Beck, A. T. 1976. *Cognitive Therapy and the Emotional Disorders*. New York: International Universities Press.

Beck, A. T., and G. Emery. 1985. *Anxiety Disorders and Phobias: A Cognitive Perspective*. New York: Basic Books.

Blanco, C., L. Bragdon, F. R. Schneier, and M. R. Liebowitz. 2014. "Psychopharmacology for Social Anxiety Disorder." In *Social Anxiety: Clinical, Developmental, and Social Perspectives* (3rd edition), edited by S. G. Hofmann and P. M. DiBartolo, 625–158. Amsterdam Elsevier/Academic Press. ISBN-13: 978-0123944276.

Blanco, C., R. G. Heimberg, F. R. Schneier, D. M. Fresco, H. Chen, C. L. Turk, et al. 2010. "A Placebo-Controlled Trial of Phenelzine, Cognitive Behavioral Group Therapy, and Their Combination for Social Anxiety Disorder." *Archives of General Psychiatry* 67: 286–95.

Brockveld, K. C., S. J. Perini, and R. M. Rapee. 2014. "Social Anxiety and Social Anxiety Disorder Across Cultures." In *Social Anxiety: Clinical, Developmental, and Social Perspectives* (3rd edition), edited by S. G. Hofmann and P. M. DiBartolo, 141–158. Amsterdam Elsevier/Academic Press. ISBN-13: 978-0123944276.

Burns, D. D. 2020. *Feeling Great*. Eau Claire, WI: PESI Publishing and Media.

Capriola-Hall, N. N., T. H. Ollendick, and S. W. White. 2021. "Attention Deployment to the Eye Region of Emotional Faces Among Adolescents with and Without Social Anxiety Disorder." *Cognitive Therapy and Research* 45: 456–467.

Clark, D. M., and A. Wells. 1995. "A Cognitive Model of Social Phobia." In *Social Phobia: Diagnosis, Assessment, and Treatment*, edited by R. G. Heimberg, M. R. Liebowitz, D. A. Hope, and F. R. Schneier, 69–93. New York: Guilford Press.

Dimberg, U., and A. Öhman. 1983. "The Effects of Directional Facial Cues on Electrodermal Conditioning to Facial Stimuli." *Psychophysiology* 20: 160–167.

Dimberg, U., M. Thunberg, and K. Elmehed. 2000. "Unconscious Facial Reactions to Emotional Facial Expressions." *Psychological Science* 11: 86–9.

Fang, A., A. T. Sawyer, A. Asnaani, and S. G. Hofmann. 2013. "Social Mishap Exposures for Social Anxiety Disorder: An Important Treatment Ingredient." *Cognitive and Behavioral Practice* 20: 213-220.

Foa, E. B., M. E. Franklin, K. J. Perry, and J. D. Herbert. 1996. "Cognitive Biases in Generalized Social Phobia." *Journal of Abnormal Psychology* 105: 433–439.

Foa, E. B., and M. J. Kozak. 1986. "Emotional Processing of Fear: Exposure to Corrective Information." *Psychological Bulletin* 99: 20–35.

Gilboa-Schechtman, E., I. Shachar, and L. Helpman. 2014. "Evolutionary Perspective on Anxiety." In *Social Anxiety: Clinical, Developmental, and Social Perspectives* (3rd edition), edited by S. G. Hofmann and P. M. DiBartolo, 599–622. Amsterdam Elsevier/Academic Press. ISBN-13: 978-0123944276.

Heimberg, R. G., C. S. Dodge, D. A. Hope, C. R. Kennedy, L. J. Zollo, and R. E. Becker. 1990. "Cognitive Behavioral Group Treatment for Social Phobia: Comparison with a Credible Placebo Control." *Cognitive Therapy and Research* 14: 1–23.

Henderson, L., P. Gilbert, and P. Zimbardo. 2014. "Shyness, Social Anxiety, and Social Phobia." In *Social Anxiety: Clinical, Developmental, and Social Perspectives* (3rd edition), edited by S. G. Hofmann and P. M. DiBartolo, 111–116. Amsterdam Elsevier/Academic Press. ISBN-13: 978-0123944276.

Hofmann, S. G. 2000. "Self-Focused Attention Before and After Treatment of Social Phobia." *Behaviour Research and Therapy* 38: 717–725.

Hofmann, S. G. 2004. "Cognitive Mediation of Treatment Change in Social Phobia." *Journal of Consulting and Clinical Psychology* 72: 392–399.

Hofmann, S. G. 2005. "Perception of Control over Anxiety Mediates the Relation Between Catastrophic Thinking and Social Anxiety in Social Phobia." *Behaviour Research and Therapy* 43: 885–895.

Hofmann, S. G. 2007. "Cognitive Factors That Maintain Social Anxiety Disorder: A Comprehensive Model and Its Treatment Implications." *Cognitive Behaviour Therapy* 36: 195–209.

Hofmann, S. G. 2014. "Interpersonal Emotion Regulation Model of Mood and Anxiety Disorders." *Cognitive Therapy and Research* 38: 483–492.

Hofmann, S. G., A. Asnaani, and D. E. Hinton. 2010. "Cultural Aspects in Social Anxiety and Social Anxiety Disorder." *Depression and Anxiety* 27: 1117–1127.

Hofmann, S. G., A. Asnaani, J. J. Vonk, A. T. Sawyer, and A. Fang. 2012. "The Efficacy of Cognitive Behavioral Therapy: A Review of Meta-Analyses." *Cognitive Therapy and Research* 36: 427–440.

Hofmann, S. G., J. K. Carpenter, and J. Curtiss. 2016. "Interpersonal Emotion Regulation Questionnaire (IERQ): Scale Development and Psychometric Characteristics." *Cognitive Therapy and Research* 40: 341–356.

Hofmann, S. G., and P. M. DiBartolo. 2000. "An Instrument to Assess Self-Statements During Public Speaking: Scale Development and Preliminary Psychometric Properties." *Behavior Therapy* 31: 499–515.

Hofmann, S. G., and S. N. Doan. 2018. *The Social Foundations of Emotion: Developmental, Cultural, and Clinical Dimensions.* Washington, D.C.: American Psychological Association. ISBN: 978-1-14338-2927-7.

Hofmann, S. G., A. Ehlers, and W. T. Roth. 1995. "Conditioning Theory: A Model for the Etiology of Public Speaking Anxiety?" *Behaviour Research and Therapy* 33: 567–571.

Hofmann, S. G., and N. Heinrichs. 2003. "Differential Effect of Mirror Manipulation on Self-Perception in Social Phobia Subtypes." *Cognitive Therapy and Research* 27: 131–142.

Hofmann, S. G., D. A. Moscovitch, H.-J. Kim, and A. N. Taylor. 2004. "Changes in Self-Perception During Treatment of Social Phobia." *Journal of Consulting and Clinical Psychology* 72: 588–596.

Hofmann S. G., and M. W. Otto. 2008. *Cognitive-Behavior Therapy of Social Anxiety Disorder: Evidence-Based and Disorder Specific Treatment Techniques.* New York: Routledge.

Hofmann, S. G., J. A. J. Smits, D. Rosenfield, N. Simon, M. W. Otto, A. E. Meuret, et al. 2013. "D-cycloserine as an Augmentation Strategy of Cognitive Behavioral Therapy for Social Anxiety Disorder." *American Journal of Psychiatry* 170: 751–758.

Johnson, S. L., B. Swerdlow, J. A. Tharp, S. Chen, J. Tackett, and J. Zeitzer. 2021. "Social Dominance and Multiple Dimensions of Psychopathology: An Experimental Test of Reactivity to Leadership and Subordinate Roles." *PLoS One* 16, no. 4 (April 28): e0250099.

Kagan, J. 2014a. "Temperamental Contributions to the Development of Psychological Profiles: I. Basic Issues." In *Social Anxiety: Clinical, Developmental, and Social Perspectives* (3rd edition), edited by S. G. Hofmann and P. M. DiBartolo, 378–418. Amsterdam Elsevier/Academic Press. ISBN-13: 978-0123944276.

Kagan, J. 2014b. "Temperamental Contributions to the Development of Psychological Profiles: II. Two Candidates." In *Social Anxiety: Clinical, Developmental, and Social Perspectives* (3rd edition), edited by S. G. Hofmann and P. M. DiBartolo, 419–443. Amsterdam Elsevier/Academic Press. ISBN-13: 978-0123944276.

Kessler, R. C., K. A. McGonagle, S. Zhao, C. B. Nelson, M. Hughes, S. Eshleman, et al. 1994. "Lifetime and 12-Month Prevalence of DSM-III-R Psychiatric Disorders in the United States: Results from the National Comorbidity Survey." *Archives of General Psychiatry* 51: 8–19.

Marks, I. M. 1987. *Fears, Phobias, and Rituals: Panic, Anxiety, and Their Disorders.* New York: Oxford University Press.

Moscovitch, D. A. 2009. "What Is the Core Fear in Social Phobia? A New Model to Facilitate Individualized Case Conceptualization and Treatment." *Cognitive and Behavioral Practice* 16: 123–134.

Moscovitch, D. A., and S. G. Hofmann. 2006. "When Ambiguity Hurts: Social Standards Moderate Self-Appraisals in Generalized Social Phobia." *Behaviour Research and Therapy* 45: 1039–1052.

Öhman, A. 1986. "Face the Beast and Fear the Face: Animal and Social Fears as Prototypes for Evolutionary Analyses of Emotion." *Psychophysiology* 23: 123–145.

Pan, J. 2019. *Sorry I'm Late, I Didn't Want to Come*. New York: Doubleday.

Phan, K. L., and H. Klumpp. 2014. "Neuroendocrinology and Neuroimaging Studies of Social Anxiety Disorder." In *Social Anxiety: Clinical, Developmental, and Social Perspectives* (3rd edition), edited by S. G. Hofmann and P. M. DiBartolo, 333–376. Amsterdam Elsevier/Academic Press. ISBN-13: 978-0123944276.

Rapee, R. M., and R. G. Heimberg. 1997. A Cognitive-Behavioral Model of Anxiety in Social Phobia. *Behaviour Research and Therapy* 35: 741–756.

Rogers, C. 1951. *Client-Centered Therapy: Its Current Practice, Implications and Theory*. London: Constable.

Schneier, F. R., L. R. Heckelman, R. Garfinkel, R. Campeas, B. Fallon, A. Gitow, et al. 1994. "Functional Impairment in Social Phobia." *Journal of Clinical Psychiatry* 55: 322–331.

Society of Clinical Psychology, Division 12, American Psychological Association. (n.d.). *Cognitive Behavioral Therapy for Social Anxiety Disorder*. https://div12.org/treatment/cognitive-behavioral-therapy-for-social-anxiety-disorder.

Solomon, R. L., and L. C. Wynne. 1953. "Traumatic Avoidance Learning: Acquisition in Normal Dogs." *Psychological Monographs: General and Applied* 67: 1–19.

Stangier, U., T. Heidenreich, M. Peitz, W. Lauterbach, and D. M. Clark. 2003. Cognitive Therapy for Social Phobia: Individual versus Group Treatment. *Behaviour Research and Therapy* 41: 991–1007.

Stein, M.B., L. J. Torgrud, and J. R. Walker. 2000. "Social Phobia Symptoms, Subtypes, and Severity: Findings from a Community Survey." *Archives of General Psychiatry* 57: 1046–1052.

Stein, M. B., J. R. Walker, and D. R. Forde. 1996. "Public Speaking Fears in a Community Sample. Prevalence, Impact on Functioning, and Diagnostic Classification." *Archives of General Psychiatry* 53: 169–174.

Trower, P. and P. Gilbert. 1989. "New Theoretical Conceptions of Social Anxiety and Social Phobia." *Clinical Psychology Review* 9: 19–35.

Turner, S. M., D. C. Beidel, M. R. Cooley, S. R. Woody, and S. C. Messer. 1994. "A Multicomponent Behavioral Treatment for Social Phobia: Social Effectiveness Therapy." *Behaviour Research and Therapy* 32: 381–390.

Williams, T., M. McCaul, G. Schwarzer, A. Cipriani, D. J. Stein, and J. Ipser. 2020. "Pharmacological Treatments for Social Anxiety Disorder in Adults: A Systematic Review and Network Meta-analysis." *Acta Neuropsychiatry* 32: 169–176.

Wong, N., D. E. Sarver, and D. C. Beidel. 2012. "Quality of Life Impairments Among Adults with Social Phobia: The Impact of Subtype." *Journal of Anxiety Disorders* 26: 50–57.

World Health Organization. 2019. *International Statistical Classification of Diseases and Related Health Problems* (11th edition). https://icd.who.int.

Stefan G. Hofmann, PhD, is one of the most widely cited experts on using cognitive behavioral therapy (CBT) for the treatment of anxiety—appearing in academic and medical journals as well as mainstream media. Hofmann has been researching social anxiety disorder for most of his career. *CBT for Social Anxiety* is the first nonprofessional book to translate Hofmann's research into a user-friendly format to help readers personalize this highly effective treatment to overcome social anxiety.

Foreword writer **Robert L. Leahy, PhD**, is author or editor of twenty-nine books, including *If Only...: Finding Freedom from Regret*, *The Worry Cure*, and *The Jealousy Cure*. He is director of the American Institute for Cognitive Therapy in New York, NY, and clinical professor of psychology at Weill Cornell Medical College.

Real change *is* possible

For more than forty-five years, New Harbinger has published proven-effective self-help books and pioneering workbooks to help readers of all ages and backgrounds improve mental health and well-being, and achieve lasting personal growth. In addition, our spirituality books offer profound guidance for deepening awareness and cultivating healing, self-discovery, and fulfillment.

Founded by psychologist Matthew McKay and Patrick Fanning, New Harbinger is proud to be an independent, employee-owned company. Our books reflect our core values of integrity, innovation, commitment, sustainability, compassion, and trust. Written by leaders in the field and recommended by therapists worldwide, New Harbinger books are practical, accessible, and provide real tools for real change.

newharbingerpublications

MORE BOOKS from
NEW HARBINGER PUBLICATIONS

THE POSITIVITY EFFECT

Simple CBT Skills to Transform Anxiety and Negativity into Optimism and Hope

978-1648481116 / US $18.95

PUT YOUR ANXIETY HERE

A Creative Guided Journal to Relieve Stress and Find Calm

978-1648481451 / US $18.95

THE ANXIETY AND PHOBIA WORKBOOK, SEVENTH EDITION

978-1684034833 / US $25.95

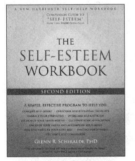

THE SELF-ESTEEM WORKBOOK, SECOND EDITION

978-1626255937 / US $22.95

MESSAGES, FOURTH EDITION

The Communication Skills Book

978-1684031719 / US $21.95

DON'T LET YOUR EMOTIONS RUN YOUR LIFE

How Dialectical Behavior Therapy Can Put You in Control

978-1572243095 / US $25.95

newharbingerpublications

1-800-748-6273 / newharbinger.com

(VISA, MC, AMEX / prices subject to change without notice)

Follow Us 🅞 f 𝕏 ▶ 🅟 📌 in

Did you know there are **free tools** you can download for this book?

Free tools are things like **worksheets, guided meditation exercises,** and **more** that will help you get the most out of your book.

You can download free tools for this book— whether you bought or borrowed it, in any format, from any source—from the New Harbinger website. All you need is a NewHarbinger.com account. Just use the URL provided in this book to view the free tools that are available for it. Then, click on the "download" button for the free tool you want, and follow the prompts that appear to log in to your NewHarbinger.com account and download the material.

You can also save the free tools for this book to your **Free Tools Library** so you can access them again anytime, just by logging in to your account! Just look for this button on the book's free tools page.

+ Save this to my free tools library